A-1 DRIVING SCHOOL

WED 5:30 - 9:30
TEST 18 + 20

POWER
UNDER CONTROL

MINISTRY OF TRANSPORTATION
AND COMMUNICATIONS ONTARIO

McClelland and Stewart Limited

© 1972 Ministry of Transportation
and Communications Ontario
In association with McClelland and Stewart

Second printing, 1973

McClelland and Stewart Limited
The Canadian Publishers
25 Hollinger Road
Toronto 374, Ontario

ISBN 0-7710-0160-6

Printed and bound in Canada

contents

preface

Power Under Control is the result of the need for a handbook for students in Driver Education classes which would be concise, attractive, and which would reflect the particular situations and rules of the Canadian driving scene. In producing this text, we have been guided by two principles. The first was that the book be useful to students all across Canada, in whatever province they may live. To that end, we have tried to make the text as wide-ranging as possible, to cover variants throughout the provinces for each situation. The second guiding principle was that of length. No longer do students appreciate bulky texts which are difficult to handle and heavy to carry. We wanted a textbook which would be easy to handle, visually pleasing, and which would convey the essentials of safe driving in a clear but concise fashion.

The compilers of the basic text are experienced teachers of high school driver education. They are:

W. H. Corner
Brantford C.I. and V.S.
Brantford

L. H. Gaffney
Mackenzie H.S.
Deep River.

R. L. Heath
Timmins H. and V.S.
Timmins

W. J. Rosenberger
Selkirk C. and V.I.
Thunder Bay

P. Salich
W. D. Lowe T. S.
Windsor

W. R. Walker
West Hill S.S.
Owen Sound

K. E. Wallace
Thomas A. Blakelock H.S.
Oakville

Eugène Hardy
Attaché d'Administration
Ministère des Transports, Québec

We also wish to thank the automobile manufacturers for their courteous assistance in providing us with research materials, as did the Alcoholism and Drug Addiction Research Foundation, the Insurance Bureau of Canada, the R.C.M.P., and the Ontario Provincial Police.

1

the car in our society

There is no such thing as a car. So what does this mean to you? What does this do to your life style?

Can you see the point we're trying to make? It is this: you could not visualize your present-day way of life, if somehow, incredibly, the automobile were suddenly subtracted from our midst. The longer you think about the consequences of such a hypothetical event, the longer becomes your list of all the ways that you would be affected.

Starting with the obvious point, most people would quickly find that their travelling range was sharply limited. The number of places they could visit, or the things that they could do, would be cut in half — at the very least. At the simplest level, the scope of interesting experiences open to most people would be greatly reduced without the widespread availability of the automobile.

Look at the problem in another way. For a great many persons, the car is the only practical means of getting to their job. Without cars, nearly everyone who now lives in suburban areas, for instance, would be unable to go to work. Something would have to change; either their work would come to them, or they would have to move. It wouldn't take much time to figure that unless the whole structure of industry were to alter, the suburbs would virtually disappear. Or to juggle slightly with the framework of our imaginary discussion, it is entirely reasonable to claim that the automobile is a major factor explaining why the suburbs are continuing to grow.

Nor does the discussion of this particular point end here. People living in suburbs want expressways that can get them to and from their job in the middle of the city in the shortest possible time. People living in the cities don't always think so much of this idea. They claim – or at least many of them do – that expressways carve up the cities and leave them ruined. Who is right? That is a question that may well turn into one of the most controversial political issues of the future.

Cars are built by people. Self-evident but significant. The automobile companies collectively are the largest employer in the industrialized world today. The largest company in the world builds cars. Three of the ten largest companies in the world build cars. It is a safe bet that the largest company in Canada builds cars. Quite obviously, cars and their manufacture are a vital component of our economy.

There's more. Besides the men who design, assemble, advertise, and sell cars, there is an almost endless succession of men and women who earn their livelihood in an occupation that is connected in some way with that one central object, the car. The miner who extracts iron ore from the ground, the smelter-worker who converts the iron to steel, the metallurgist who decides the exact composition of the steel according to what function it must perform – these persons operate at the beginning of the process. The chemist who synthesizes artificial rubber for the tires, or invents a new plastic for the tail light, is equally involved in the creation of the automobile.

How about the engineer who designs the highways and bridges we drive on? How about the truckers carrying gravel to the construction site, or the pavers who finish off the asphalt surface? Don't forget the geologist who searches for crude oil, or the well-driller who brings it to the surface, or the engineer whose pipe lines bring it to the refinery, or the other engineer who separates the crude oil into gasoline, oil, grease, and related products.

Driving instructors depend on the car for their living. So do gas-jockeys, mechanics, rust-prevention appliers, chauffeurs, racing-car drivers, taxi-drivers, truck-drivers, and countless dozens of other drivers. Tax collectors, traffic policemen, lawyers, and judges all have the car to thank for some portion of their income. Accessory manufacturers produce anything from fancy hubcaps to stereo tapedecks. Finally, at the end of the cycle, there is the auto-wrecker. The next person on the scene is the car-salesman again. . . .

One in six Canadians works in a job directly or indirectly connected with the automobile, and one in seven Canadian businesses is directly or indirectly involved with automobile manufacture. If the automobile were suddenly to disappear, the economic consequences would be utterly impossible to predict.

Our dependence on the automobile is the root of two particularly worrisome problems presently facing our society.

Problem one is that automobiles damage the environment. The fear of a future landscape completely covered with asphalt paving is a topic not restricted to science-fiction writers. Automobile junkyards and roadside billboards could only be called beautiful by those who are making money from them.

But these are not the real concerns. By far the most immediate and serious worry posed by our involvement with the automobile is the now-familiar danger of air pollution. The petroleum-based fuels used by car engines emit small quantities of carbon monoxide, nitrous oxide, and other gases, as well as unburnt hydrocarbon particles and lead. Given the tremendous number of cars being driven every day, a small amount of pollution from each one adds up to a formidable concentration of dirty air, especially in the cities. When this concentration is aggravated by unfavourable atmospheric conditions, the total effect can be alarming indeed.

Despite the danger that exists, considerable progress has been made towards controlling the pollution problem. The introduction of cleaner-burning gasoline is one advance. Changes in engine-design have made cars a good deal cleaner than they used to be. Totally new types of powerplants are being introduced on an experimental basis. Perhaps as important a change as any is that public awareness of the problem now exists, so that air pollution is no longer ignored or tolerated.

The second major problem of the automobile is that it is dangerous. Every hour someone in North America is killed in a car accident and twenty-five persons are injured. In Canada, over five thousand persons are killed each year. More North Americans have been killed in automobiles than in wars – by far. These are incredible statistics if you stop to think about them.

What can be done about this highly unpleasant side-effect of the car? The problem can be tackled in a number of ways. One approach is that of improved highway design. Better lighting, better signs, better intersection control, less rigid light standards and guard rails, and other improvements have all contributed to a less painful accident-per-mile figure than might otherwise have been the case.

Another approach –and one which has aroused a great deal of controversy – is to improve the design of the car from the point of view of safety. Unquestionably, great steps forward have been taken. Fifteen years ago, seat belts were an oddity; now, belts as well as shoulder harnesses are standard equipment in every car and, with their value proven beyond all doubt, are actually being worn, rather than stuck behind the seat as a dust-gathering nuisance. Protruding switches and knobs have been removed from the car interior, and replaced by padded dashboards. On the outside of the car, sharp tailfins, hood ornaments, and hubcaps are gone.

Despite these measures, "consumer protection" groups have been outspoken in their criticism of the manufacturers, whom they accuse of dragging their heels, being more concerned with designing glamour into their cars than safety features. The manufacturers, in reply, state that safety features are fairly expensive to add, and have been proven to have very little sales appeal. Therefore, any manufacturer who took the lead in safety improvements would find that his profits were cut – which in fact has happened, in at least one case. Given the fact that they are obliged to pay satisfactory dividends to their shareholders, the manufacturers not surprisingly are opposed to any change that threatens to decrease their profits.

Does this make you indignant that the car manufacturers are going slow on safety improvements? You are wrong. By and large, the car companies have been agreeable to accept government-imposed safety standards. The reason for this is that *all* manufacturers will have to incorporate similar changes, and none will suffer a competitive disadvantage. Despite this acceptance, however, there has still been some resistance by the manufacturers, on the grounds that some of the government standards are too tough to be met in the time allowed.

"Why build better highways and safer cars when the real problem underlying the accident statistics is still the same as ever – the nut behind the wheel?"

The above quotation is an old, perhaps rather irritating, opinion about the causes of traffic accidents. Nevertheless, innumerable objective studies have all pointed to the same conclusion – that the greatest single cause of accidents is, in fact, the driver. The reasons for this vary with the circumstances – in one case, the problem may be lack of driving skill; in another, a momentary lapse of attention. Or poor vision. Or failure to compensate for bad conditions. Or intoxication. Or over-confidence. Or a combination of several of these, or a different reason altogether. But these are problems we ourselves can correct – and that is the whole point of this chapter and this book. Anyone can learn to drive. But expert driving – and, really, safe driving is exactly the same thing – is a skill that takes more time to acquire, and has as its benefits the pleasure and satisfaction that come from doing any task properly. The rest of this book is just a post-script to this single point.

2

getting your driver's licence

One of the high points of your life is the moment you obtain your driver's licence. A whole new range of experiences suddenly becomes possible, from the simple pleasure of driving itself, to the purely practical aspects of performing useful functions that otherwise could never even be attempted. Most people are eager to obtain their licence just as soon as they reach the legal age for driving. It must always be remembered, however, that driving a car is a privilege, not a right. Misuse of this privilege can result in your licence being revoked or suspended. No one may drive a motor vehicle on a public road unless he holds a valid licence.

Even before you get behind the wheel, the first step is to learn the traffic laws, the meaning of the road-signs, and the rules of the road. A good way to begin is to obtain a *Driver's Handbook* or manual from your provincial licence-issuing authority. Study it carefully. It will tell you in simple language the traffic laws of your province and how to get — and keep — your licence.

In most provinces the minimum age at which you can obtain a driver's licence is sixteen, but in some provinces the minimum age is seventeen, while in others you may drive a motor-scooter or motorcycle at a lower age than you can drive a car.

There are various types of driver's licences. In addition to an ordinary driver's licence, some provinces require you to have a special licence to drive a motorcycle, an ambulance, a taxi, truck, bus, school bus, or a farm truck. If you have to wear glasses when driving, or have a disability which could possibly require special equipment on your car, you may have to take a special driving test. When driving in some foreign countries, you may be required to obtain an International Driver's Licence. Information on the different types of licences can be obtained from your provincial licensing authority.

REQUIREMENTS FOR DRIVER'S LICENCE	B.C.	ALTA.	SASK.	MAN.	ONT.	QUE.	N.B.	N.S.	P.E.I.	NFLD.
Minimum Age	16	16	16	16	16	17*	16	16	16	17
Age at which written consent of parent or guardian is required	16 to 21	under 18	under 18	under 18	under 17	under 18	under 18	under 18	None required	
Vision test required	Yes	Yes	Yes	Yes	Yes	Yes	Yes	Yes	Yes	No
Rules-of-the-road test required — written or oral	Written	Both	Both	Both	Both	Both	Both	Both	Both	Written
Sign-recognition test required — written or oral	Oral	Both	Both	Both	Both	Written	Both	Both	Written	Oral
Road test required	Yes	Yes	Yes	Yes	Yes	Yes	Yes	Yes	Yes	Yes

*16 if applicant has had a driver education course

THE INSTRUCTION PERMIT

Once you have carefully studied the *Driver's Handbook*, the next step is to obtain an instruction permit. This entitles you to drive a motor vehicle provided that you are accompanied by a licensed driver. You may not drive a car alone on a highway with just an instruction permit — you must be accompanied by a qualified driver at all times.

An instruction permit is only valid for a short period of time. If it expires before you successfully complete your driver examination, you must renew it if you wish to continue to practise driving. Don't forget to sign your permit!

Before you receive your instruction permit, you must pass several preliminary tests. These will probably include a vision test; a test on the rules of the road, which may be oral, written, or both; and a sign-recognition test, which again may be oral, written, or both.

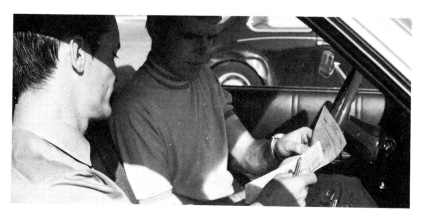

THE ROAD TEST

After you have practised driving with your instructor and you feel qualified to drive safely, the next step is to take your road test. The driver examiner will accompany you in your car and will ask you to carry out various manoeuvres which will be a test of your skill as a driver. These may include starting from the curb; parallel parking; stopping, parking, and starting on a grade; backing; driving along; and other procedures.

The examiner will also watch to see if you take correct precautions at intersections, railroad crossings, and left and right turns; if you show proper awareness of other traffic; and if you recognize and obey signs, signals, and pavement markings. By the time the test is finished, the examiner will have a clear indication as to whether or not you have learned to handle a motor vehicle with a reasonable degree of skill and safety.

If you are successful in passing your test you will be issued with your driver's licence. Be sure to sign it immediately. If you change your home address you must inform the licensing authority, and if you move to another province you must exchange your old licence for a new one of the province you are now living in. You will not be required to take another driver's test unless your licence has a restriction on it. It is illegal to hold licences from more than one province at the same time. It is also illegal to lend your licence to another person.

In some provinces, probationary licences are issued to all new drivers. In these cases, you must drive for a period of time, usually twelve months, without any violation or accident, before a full driver's licence is issued to you. If you do commit a violation or have an accident during the probationary period, your licence may be suspended or your probationary period extended. It seems likely that more provinces will be utilizing probationary licences in the future.

You may feel that the licensing authorities go to a lot of trouble before they issue a driver's licence, and this is true. This is because so many new drivers are involved in accidents on our highways. The driver examiners do their utmost to ensure that only drivers who are skilled and can handle a motor vehicle safely are given a licence to drive.

The following table gives a breakdown of all road accidents by age groups.

Road Accidents In Canada

Age Group	Number of Accidents	Percentage of Total
Under 16 (illegal)	1,568	.4
16 – 24	153,220	33.5
25 – 34	107,145	23.4
35 – 44	83,100	18.1
45 – 54	60,435	13.2
55 – 64	35,166	7.7
65 and over	16,854	3.7

As you see from the table, the age group 16-24 is involved in one-third of all road accidents in Canada. It should also be borne in mind that, on the average, drivers in this category drive fewer miles than persons in the higher age groups, since the latter groups contain numerous long-distance truck drivers, commercial travellers, and many others who drive for a living.

It is in an effort to reduce this disproportionate level of accidents that driver education courses are being offered in so many second-ary schools in Canada. Nowadays, a car is so simple to manipulate that anyone can learn to start, steer, and stop a car in a very short period of time. Because of their youth, alert minds, and fast reflexes, young people quickly become skilled in the mechanics of driving. They should be the best and safest drivers on our roads today. But the accident statistics prove that they are not, and this is what driver education is all about.

Why? Why should this be? The answer, really, is simple enough, but it's the kind of answer that people often find hard to listen to, because it may seem unimportant, over-rated, or old-fashioned. If you stop to think about it, though, nothing could be more mistaken. *The vital key to safe driving is a safe attitude.* This is the most important asset any driver, young or old, can have. A desire to drive safely and well, a concern for other vehicles on the highway, a concern for pedestrians who may be young and thoughtless, or old and infirm – these are the things that make up our attitude to driving and determine whether we shall have years of pleasant and happy driving, or whether we may spend years in useless remorse over an accident which need never have happened.

Skilled, safe operation of a car is an accomplishment which can bring tremendous satisfaction to a driver, and in the following chapters of this book it is hoped that you will learn from the experts just how important it is. When you get your first driver's licence you have satisfied the driver examiner that you know how to operate a motor vehicle safely, but there is so much more to handling the many traffic problems you will meet! A correct attitude to driving will help you to meet these problems safely, to anticipate them, and to avoid them before it is too late.

Remember: Driving is a privilege, not a right.

3

meet your wheels

OCCUPANT-PROTECTION EQUIPMENT

The safety and protection of you and your passengers are of vital importance. During recent years federal and provincial legislation has demanded that car manufacturers build safety devices in the automobile. Many such features have been incorporated, and more will be added in the future.

The driver must be comfortable in the seat, and be able to reach and see all the controls. The seat can be adjusted by moving a lever found under the front or at the side of the seat. Most drivers prefer to sit directly behind the steering wheel, with enough space to allow their arms to move freely while turning. The seat should not be so far back, however, that you have to stretch your feet to reach the pedals.

Seat belts are standard equipment on all new vehicles. Some are spring-tensioned, while others require manual adjustment. Some vehicles have a red warning-light on the dash to remind the driver to fasten the seat belts before pulling away. In addition to the seat belts, shoulder harnesses also hold the driver against the seat and protect him from an impact force. The harnesses are attached above the front side-windows of the car, and hook up to part of the seat belt. It is important that seat belts and shoulder harnesses be correctly worn with lap belt snug and low over the pelvic bone, shoulder belt

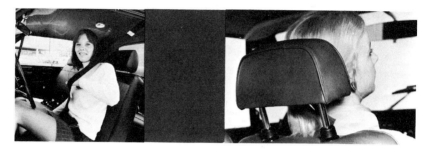

slack — a fist's width away from the chest. Properly adjusted, belts and harnesses are not only an important safety factor but can also increase the pleasure of driving by holding the driver comfortably in position. And remember — belts and harnesses should *always* be fastened, for a short drive around the block as much as for a long journey across the country.

A padded instrument panel and dash help to reduce injury in the event of a crash, since the padding acts as a cushion under impact. Padded sunvisors cut glare from the sun or the road, and also reduce injury in accidents. They can usually be swung to the side, and can be adjusted to relieve eye strain, while still allowing a sufficiently wide angle-of-vision for safe driving. Visors should be placed in the normal position when leaving the car.

Headrests guard against whiplash injuries, by preventing an occupant's head from being thrown back violently during a crash. If adjustable, they should be set at the correct height to meet the back of the head, and not used as a head support while driving.

Doors should always be locked when you are driving, so as to prevent the occupants from being thrown from the car in the event of an accident. Some cars have a "lock-warning light" to remind the driver if his door is not locked when the car is moving.

Padded instrument panel

Ventilation vents allow fresh air to enter the interior of the car. One vent or window should be kept open slightly to keep fresh air in the car. Carbon monoxide is odourless, tasteless, and colourless, and may enter the car through the fire wall, floor, or any small opening. Avoid travelling too closely behind a vehicle emitting excessive fumes, since these may be drawn in through the vents.

Recent developments by auto manufacturers in the field of automotive safety include collapsible steering-columns, interior door-beams, and recessed knobs. A collapsible steering-column crushes at a controlled rate under impact in order to minimize chest injuries. Interior door-beams are welded inside the door panels for added strength — a valuable safety feature in the event of a side collision. Recessed knobs reduce head injuries in situations in which occupants are thrown against the instrument panel.

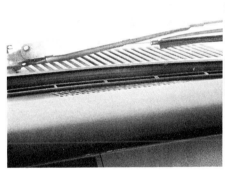

Ventilation vents

Collapsible steering-column

SEE AND BE SEEN

Illumination

Good lights light your way to safety. They are a form of defence as well as an aid to good driving.

The major lights on an automobile are the headlights, front parking lights, tail lights, and brake lights.

Headlight systems consist of either two or four headlights, with each system having a high and a low beam. All cars have a control switch for changing from high beam to low beam and vice versa; this "dimmer switch," as it is called, is located on the floorboard to the left of the brake or clutch (on North American cars) or on the steering column (on many European and Japanese cars). Headlights must be dimmed for oncoming traffic at 500 feet. When approaching another car from behind, lights must be dimmed at 200 feet. A few cars have an electronic headlight dimmer-switch which automatically controls the beam-setting according to traffic conditions.

The light switch controls the headlights, dash lights, tail lights, licence plate lights, and the front parking lights. On most cars the front amber parking lights and the red tail lights stay on when the headlights are on. Driving with parking lights only is illegal after dark.

The brake lights are not controlled by a manual switch, but operate automatically whenever the brakes are applied. They emit a brilliant red glow that warns drivers in following cars to slow down or stop.

In addition to the major lights discussed above, there are important minor lights as well. These include cornering lights, which illuminate the road by the front fender on either a left or right turn; the lights for the glove compartment, for under the hood, and for the trunk. All interior lights other than those for the instruments should be off when the car is moving.

Signals

Directional signals are used to indicate to others the direction of a turn or lane change you wish to make. The control lever is located on the left side of the steering column behind the steering wheel. Signal-indicator lights, which remind the driver that his signal is on, are located on the dash. An alert driver always uses the correct signal at the proper time, and allows extra time on expressways. Never forget your turn signal — without it, other drivers may not be able to react fast enough when you change direction.

The four-way warning-light switch is located on the dash or steering column. When activated, the front signal lights and the rear signal lights flash on and off to act as a warning device. This signal is used when the car is stopped for any emergency.

Side marker-lights or reflectors warn other drivers of the position of a vehicle, whether parked or moving. The lights or reflectors are located on the front and rear fenders of each side of the car.

Back-up lights illuminate the area behind the car when backing at night. The lights automatically go on when the car is in reverse.

Rear view mirror   *Side mirror*

Mirrors

The interior rear view mirror reflects through the rear window to indicate the area behind the car. Some mirrors of this type have a "day-night" switch; the night side of the mirror reduces the headlight glare of a following vehicle. A side mirror reflects the area to the rear on the driver's side. On some cars these mirrors are remote controlled from the inside; on others they must be adjusted from the outside. Mirrors should be kept clean and in correct adjustment.

A "blind spot" is an area that is obstructed from view by the car itself. Mirrors reduce these blind-spot areas, but do not completely eliminate them. A good driver always checks the mirrors frequently to review the traffic situation, and looks quickly over his shoulder to check on traffic or obstacles in his blind spots.

SAFETY INSTRUMENTS

The Horn

Used properly, one of the most important safety aids is the horn. Better than any other means, the horn serves to warn other drivers of a dangerous situation that they might not be aware of. By the same token, however, the horn when used improperly can be intensely irritating, and can thus be a hazard rather than a safeguard. Never be inconsiderate when using the horn.

The horn is operated by pressing the horn rim or the centre of the steering wheel, depending on the car. Remember: tap the horn — don't lean on it!

Windshield Wipers

Windshield wipers remove rain, dirt, sleet, and snow from the windshield to keep it clear. For best results, wiper blades should be kept clean. Always wet the windshield with the windshield washers before turning the wipers on if it is not raining or snowing — grit on dry glass wears out the wiper blades. During the winter months the wiper blades should be freed from any ice on the windshield before using. Winter wiper blades are heavier than the standard blade, and have a covering which helps to prevent ripping in ice and snow conditions. Most modern cars have electric two- or three-speed wipers. Low speeds are used for light rain or drizzle, medium and high speeds for moderate to heavy rain and snow.

To help the wipers function more efficiently, most cars are equipped with windshield washers, which emit a spray of water or solvent on the windshield. The control for operating the washers is usually part of the wiper switch, or a separate switch beside it. The solvent is in a container under the hood. Check the level frequently, and be sure to use a cold-weather solvent containing anti-freeze during the winter.

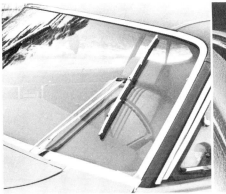

Wipers   *Washer control*

The Heater-Defroster System

The heater-defroster supplies hot or cold air to the interior of the car. The controls are located on the dash. The front defroster is at the bottom of the windshield inside the car, and the heater is under the dash close to the floor. Most heater-defroster units have variable controls to regulate the amount and temperature of hot or cold air produced, or even to adjust the direction of the air flow. Some cars are also equipped with a rear-window defroster and heater.

Some cars are equipped with air-conditioning units. These units operate similarly to a heater-defroster except that they have vents and a temperature dial which determines and maintains the desired temperature. All windows should be closed when the air-conditioning unit is operating.

Gauges

Gauges or instruments are necessary for indicating the speed, pressures, temperature, and capacities of various parts of the vehicle. Each has a specific function, and should be checked constantly while driving. All the gauges are situated close together on the instrument panel so that they can easily be read.

A speedometer indicates the speed at which the vehicle is moving. Some have coloured divisions, for night driving, such as green to 30 miles per hour, amber for 30 to 50 miles per hour, and red for over 50 miles per hour. In the centre of the speedometer is another instrument called the "odometer," which records the number of miles the car has travelled since manufacture. A few cars come equipped with "trip odometers," which can easily be reset to zero; these are useful for measuring the distance of individual journeys.

Tachometers show the revolutions-per-minute of the engine crankshaft. These are usually found on sports cars.

An ammeter is a device for indicating the condition of the electrical power-supply for the car. In some cars, the ammeter is a gauge; in other cars, it is a warning light. A zero reading on the gauge indicates no charge or discharge; a minus reading indicates a discharge; a plus reading indicates a charge. For cars with warning lights, a red light indicates a discharge; otherwise, the electrical system is charging or is neutral. If a discharge shows at normal driving speed, have the system checked.

Oil pressure may also be indicated by either a gauge or a warning light. These instruments indicate the oil *pressure* in the engine; they do not indicate the oil *level*. On a gauge, the correct reading at normal operating temperature is 15-to-25 pounds pressure while idling, and 40-to-50 pounds pressure at driving speed. With a warning light, a red glow indicates dangerously low oil pressure. If this happens, stop the vehicle and engine immediately and have the system checked. It may help to add more oil, but be careful not to overfill the crankcase. The correct level is indicated by the "full" line on the dipstick.

The temperature indicator measures the temperature of the coolant (that is, the water or the anti-freeze) in the engine. This is done by means of a gauge, a red light, or a red and green light. Normal temperature is usually between 160 and 195 degrees. If the gauge goes above 200 degrees or the red light comes on under normal driving conditions, stop the vehicle and engine immediately and have the system checked. Use extreme caution when checking a hot engine.

The fuel gauge indicates the quantity of gasoline in the gas tank. The tank should be refilled when the gauge reads one-quarter full. Don't be caught — it may be a long walk to the next service station!

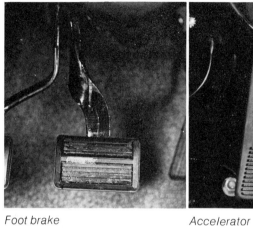

Foot brake

Accelerator

Parking brake and release

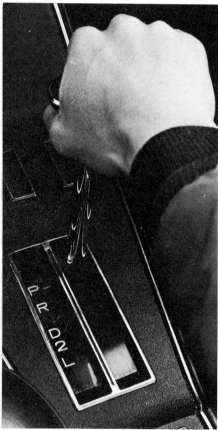

Manual gearshift

Automatic gearshift

THE MAIN CONTROLS

The main controls are probably the most important parts of a car, since they enable the driver to start, stop, change speed, and change direction. It is extremely important, therefore, that the driver be completely familiar with the location and function of all the controls, and be able to reach and operate each one easily and immediately.

The Steering Wheel

The steering wheel is used for changing a car's direction. The driver's hands should be on the outside of the wheel in the "ten-and-two" position. It is extremely important always to keep both hands on the wheel; if you hit a sudden bump, one hand alone may not be enough to keep control of the vehicle.

The Accelerator

The accelerator regulates the speed of the vehicle. It is operated by the right pedal at the driver's feet. A few cars are equipped with an automatic cruise control, which will keep the car at a specific speed. The cruise control releases when the brakes or accelerator are applied. The switch or knob for this device is located on the dash.

The Foot Brake

The foot brake is used to slow down or stop the car. It is operated by a pedal to the left of the accelerator. Always use your right foot on the brake. (There are at least six good reasons for this practice – how many can you think of?) The amount of pressure necessary to operate the brakes may vary with different cars – power brakes are usually much more sensitive than regular brakes, for instance – so it is a good idea to test the brakes on an unfamiliar car before driving at normal speed. Though power brakes are more sensitive, they do not help you to stop any more quickly.

The Parking Brake

The parking brake, unlike the foot brake, stays on until released by the driver. It is used to stop the car from rolling backwards on a hill, and should also be left on when the car is parked. (It should be remembered, however, that the parking brake is not as strong as the regular brake; if you park on a steep hill, follow the procedures indicated in Chapter 7.) The parking brake may also be used in an emergency if the foot brake fails. The two common types of parking brake are the hand type, located under the dash, and the floor type with the foot pedal at the extreme left of the floorboard. For the floor type, the driver pushes the pedal down with the left foot to put the brake on, and pulls the brake-release knob out to release it. Some cars have a red warning-light on the dash which glows when the parking brake is on.

The Gearshift

There are two basic types of gearshift: the automatic and the manual. The great majority of cars produced in North America have automatics, and since these are considerably easier for learning to drive, at this stage of the book we shall refer only to this type of gearshift. The manual transmission is discussed in Chapter 21 near the end of the book.

The automatic gearshift selects the desired forward or reverse gears, and when in the Park position, locks the transmission to prevent the car from rolling if there is a slope. Depending on the type of car, the gearshift control is located on the dash, on the steering column behind the steering wheel, or on the console. The gear selector is illuminated for night driving. Some automatic transmissions have two forward speeds, while others have three or four.

For normal forward driving, the Drive position is always used. The Low position may be used when driving up or down a steep grade, especially under icy, slippery conditions. For backing up, the vehicle must be brought to a full stop before putting the gearshift in Reverse. The car should never be in Neutral when going down a hill, since the vehicle will not have any braking support from the engine. This is a dangerous practice.

The Choke

The choke supplies a rich gasoline mixture to the carburetor, and is used when starting a cold engine. All modern North American cars have an automatic choke, which regulates the air-fuel mixture automatically. Some imported cars and trucks have a manual choke, which is operated by a knob on the dash. For starting a cold engine, a manual choke should be pulled out, and gradually pushed in as the engine warms up. Do not use the manual choke when the engine is warm.

Choke   *Ignition*

The Ignition

Each car is supplied with two keys. The ignition key is used to start the car and open the doors, and the trunk key opens the trunk and the glove compartment.

The ignition switch is located on the dash or steering column. Most switches have four positions: accessory, off, on, and start. The "accessory" position is used when playing the radio, etc., with the engine stopped. The "start" position is for starting the engine. The "on" position is for all operations with the engine running, and of course, the "off" position stops the engine and most accessories.

On most modern cars, the ignition switch also has an anti-theft warning buzzer. If the key is left in the ignition when the doors are opened, the buzzer sounds in order to remind the driver to remove the key and lock the doors. Always lock your car — but always remember to check first, to make sure your keys aren't inside!

Before you actually begin to drive the car, it is an excellent idea to spend a short period of time just sitting behind the wheel, familiarizing yourself with all the controls and how they work. You should be able to operate any control instantly without looking at it — especially the main controls such as the brake, gearshift, accelerator, and steering wheel. Once you are able to do this, you will be ready to begin practice driving with your instructor.

4

move your wheels

PRE-STARTING

Once you are completely familiar with your vehicle, you are ready to begin. Before pulling away in your car, however, be sure that it is completely safe for driving. Here is a list of points you should always check before starting the engine:

1. All books and coats should be placed in the trunk, so that you have a greater amount of room available for driving unhampered — a safety feature and a comfort feature combined.
2. Be sure that the rear deck of the car is clear. If you stop suddenly, any loose articles on the rear deck could be hurled to the front, and injury may result.
3. You should get into the car by the curb side whenever practicable. In some provinces it is an offence to open the driver's door in any way that creates a hazard to passing vehicles. In automobiles in which this is impractical, or in awkward situations, extreme care must be taken. Always approach the driver's-side door from the front of the car, so that you cannot fail to see oncoming traffic.
4. All doors should be locked to help prevent them from flying open in a collision, and to keep anyone from forcing his way into your car if you stop in traffic.

5. Check to ensure that the parking brake is on to prevent any movement of the vehicle. The gear selector should be in Park before starting.

6. Make sure that the signal lights function properly. (In some cars, the ignition key may have to be switched on before they will work.) If they do not, hand signals must be used.

7. Adjust the ventilation; excessive heat will cause drowsiness, and poor ventilation may create a carbon-monoxide hazard.

8. Adjust the seat so that you can reach all foot pedals comfortably. Also make sure that you have unobstructed vision at all angles. It may be necessary to use cushions to attain this.

9. Adjust all mirrors so that you can tell at a glance the positions of other vehicles on the road.

10. *Fasten Seat Belts*. Statistics have proven that the "second collision" (between the occupants of the car and the inside of the car itself) is the injury-producing situation. It is your responsibility as driver to check that all safety belts are being used – yours as well as the passengers'. The car should not be put in motion until all belts are fastened and adjusted.

11. Check that the brake pedal has resistance when you press it. This indicates that there is sufficient brake fluid in the brake lines and that the brakes will function properly. If the hydraulic brakes do not function, do not attempt to get to a garage, but have the car towed there by a tow truck.

12. Be alert but relaxed. You are no longer a pedestrian. You are in command of a powerful machine that can give thousands of miles of service and satisfaction, but which is also capable of destroying life and property.

STARTING UP

Cars vary greatly in starting procedure; the correct method for one might not work with another. Starting procedures will also vary with the weather, a fact which must be taken into consideration. The procedure outlined below is suitable with most cars; it is advisable, however, to consult the owner's manual for your own car first.

1. Press the accelerator part way down and hold it in position. In cold weather, it is recommended that the accelerator be completely depressed, and then allowed to return to its normal

starting position. For this step especially, there is considerable variation between different cars, so you should consult the owner's manual for further details.

2. Turn the key to the "on" position. A glance at the instrument panel will show if all the indicator lights and gauges are functioning.

3. Turn the key to the "start" position. Release the key as soon as the engine starts — it will automatically return to the correct position. If the starter is held or re-engaged, damage to the starter mechanism may result.

4. Release the pressure on the accelerator so that the engine does not turn over too quickly. Allow the engine to idle for a short time.

5. Re-check the instrument panel. The oil indicator-light should be out, or, if a gauge, should show pressure. The ammeter light should also be out or the gauge should show a charge. The parking brake should be on.

PREPARING TO DRIVE

Are you emotionally prepared to drive? Are you ready to concentrate all your attention on driving? Do you possess the necessary safe attitude for competent, efficient driving? Are you willing to overlook the mistakes of other drivers? If the answers to all of these questions are "yes," then you are ready to begin.

At this stage, of course, you are still driving in a practice area; once the basic skills and principles have been mastered, it will be time to begin driving in actual traffic conditions.

1. Make sure the parking brake is on.

2. Press the brake pedal with the right foot and hold. The vehicle must not move until you are ready. This step also tests the brakes for proper functioning, and is an excellent safety precaution. If the brake is working properly, you will be unable to press the pedal completely to the floor.

3. Move the selector lever to Drive. This is the position for normal driving in most cars.

4. Place your hands on the steering wheel in the "ten-and-two" position.

5. Always look behind you. Using the mirrors is not enough: there is a "blind spot" that must be checked by looking over your left shoulder.
6. Signal your intentions, to inform other drivers what you intend to do. (Even at this practice stage, you should perform every step as though you were in regular traffic. This way, the proper techniques will soon become second nature, and you will make the transition from the practice area to the busy street with a minimum of difficulty.)
7. Remove your right foot from the brake and place it on the accelerator. Your left foot should be used only to engage the parking brake and to change the driving lights from low to high and back.
8. Release the parking brake.
9. Gently depress the accelerator. Smooth driving is the mark of the expert.

10. Re-check the traffic, and move out when the way is clear. Always re-check traffic. You are now on the road. Look ahead and get the complete picture. Know what is behind you, to your left, to your right, and in front.
11. In preparing to stop, check your blind spot, signal, and then pull over to the side of the road when the way is clear.
12. Brake to a smooth stop. Place the gear selector in Park, turn off the ignition, and remove the key. Engage the parking brake, and, if leaving the car, lock all doors. Leave via the curb side if at all possible.

PRACTICE MANOEUVRES

When you have become familiar with the car and the sequences required for starting and stopping, practise the following manoeuvres, moving from Exercise One to Nine. During the exercises, good driving habits will be formed by remembering to use the proper signalling and "shoulder checking" techniques at all times.

Use a parking lot or an off-street area to practise in, if possible, and if stanchions or some other kind of markers are available, they will also prove very helpful.

When you are driving, remember to make all your movements gently, using light pressure on the accelerator or the brake pedal, and easy movements of the steering wheel. A good driver is a smooth driver.

When you are ready, start the car and move away slowly.

Exercise One: Driving Forward In A Straight Line

— Make sure the parking brake is on.
— With your right foot on the brake, place the gear selector in Drive.
— Keep your hands on the steering wheel at the "ten-and-two" position.
— Check the traffic.
— Signal.
— Place your right foot on the accelerator.
— Release the parking brake.
— Press gently on the accelerator, so that you move ahead slowly.

— Remove your right foot from the accelerator and apply the brake easing up slightly just before the car comes to a stop.
— Move the gear selector to Park.

Exercise Two: Backing In A Straight Line

— With your right foot on the brake, move the gear selector to the Reverse position.
— Assume the proper backing position (see diagram).
— Check the traffic.
— Place your right foot on the accelerator, and back very slowly in a straight line.
— Replace your right foot on the brake, and bring the car to a gentle stop.
— Move the gear selector to Park.

Exercise Three: Steering Left And Right

TURNING LEFT

— Place your hands at the "ten-and-two" position on the steering wheel.
— Turn the wheel counter-clockwise with the right hand.
— Cross your left hand *over* your right, and, grasping the wheel at the top, pull it downwards to the left.
— Replace your right hand at the two o'clock position, and turn counter-clockwise again.
— Straighten your wheels as you complete your turn by letting the steering wheel slide through your hands. Be prepared to correct as needed.

TURNING RIGHT
— Place your hands at the ten-and-two position.
— Turn the wheel clockwise with your left hand.
— Cross your right hand *over* your left, and, grasping the wheel at the top, pull it downwards to the right.
— Replace your left hand at the ten o'clock position, and turn clockwise again.
— Straighten your wheels as when turning left.

When you practise these manoeuvres, be sure the car is moving before you begin to turn the steering wheel; otherwise, excessive wear to the tires and the steering mechanism will result.

When straightening out from a curve, return the steering wheel to its original position in a hand-over-hand motion. If your speed is over ten miles per hour, *most* cars will straighten themselves automatically. Loosen your grip, so that the steering wheel can slip through your hands until the car is heading straight again. Always be careful when using this technique, however; *never remove your hands from the steering wheel*, and always be prepared to use the hand-over-hand method if the car is not straightening quickly enough. Also remember that some cars — especially those with power steering — require the hand-over-hand method to straighten out.

Exercise Four: Turning A Corner To The Right

— Drive slowly forward.
— Signal a right turn.
— Check your mirrors, and over your right shoulder.
— Adjust your speed before starting the turn (braking in the turn can cause a skid).
— Take your foot off the brake and return it to the accelerator. Maintain speed, but do not accelerate.
— Turn the steering wheel to the right, using the techniques from Exercise Three. Be careful not to oversteer.
— Straighten your wheels as you complete your turn by letting the steering wheel slide through your hands. Be prepared to correct as needed.
— Accelerate lightly coming out of the turn. *Caution*: harsh acceleration in the turn may cause a skid.

Left hand signals right turn
Right hand in position to start right turn

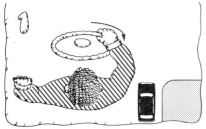

Left hand takes position on wheel
and applies turning power

Right hand
releases at
bottom of its
turn

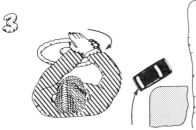

Left hand continues turning while
right hand crosses over it to the top
of the wheel

Right hand
takes position at top of wheel and
applies final turning power. Left
hand releases at bottom of its turn

Exercise Five: Turning A Corner To The Left

— Drive slowly forward.
— Signal a left turn.
— Check your mirrors, and over your left shoulder.
— Adjust your speed before starting the turn.
— Take your foot off the brake and return it to the accelerator.
  Maintain speed but do not accelerate.
— Turn the steering wheel to the left.
— Straighten your wheels as you complete your turn by letting the
  steering wheel slide through your hands. Be prepared to correct
  as needed.
— Accelerate lightly coming out of the turn.

Exercise Six: Making A Figure-8 Turn

The purpose of a figure-8 turn is to combine right and left turns in the same exercise. Figure-8 turns may be made either starting to the left or to the right—both should be practised. *Caution*: this manoeuvre should be practised only in a vacant parking lot or other open space.
– Drive slowly forward.
– Signal a right turn.
– Check your mirrors, and over your right shoulder.
– Turn the steering wheel to the right. Complete a 360-degree turn before straightening out.
– Signal a left turn.
– Check your mirrors and over your left shoulder.
– Turn the steering wheel left. Complete a 360-degree turn before straightening out.
– Repeat the procedure several times. Try varying the sharpness of your turns, so as to make large 8's and small 8's.

Exercise Seven: Backing To The Right

– Place the gear selector in Reverse.
– Assume the proper backing position. Many drivers find the best procedure is to place their left hand on the steering wheel at the 12 o'clock position, shift their position in the seat, and look backwards over their right shoulder.
– Back the car very slowly.

Clockwise

Counterclockwise

Backing

Backing

— Turn the wheel clockwise to the right (the rear of the car will turn right).
— Just before the car has reached a 90-degree turn, straighten the car by steering to the left.
— Apply the brake to stop the car gently.
— Return the gear selector to the Park position. *Caution*: since vision is restricted when backing, a good rule to follow is never to back unless necessary, and never back farther than necessary.

Exercise Eight: Backing To The Left

— Place the gear selector in Reverse.
— Back the car very slowly.
— Place hands at the ten-and-two position on the steering wheel. Turn the wheel counter-clockwise to the left (the rear of the car will turn left).
— Just before the car has completed a 90-degree turn, straighten the car by steering to the right.
— Apply the brakes to stop the car gently.
— Return the gear selector to the Park position.

Exercise Nine: Backing The Car Through A Figure-8 Turn

— Place the gear selector in Reverse.
— Back the car very slowly.
— Place both hands at the ten-and-two position on the steering wheel. Turn to the right (clockwise). After the car has completed a 360-degree turn, turn the wheel to the left and straighten the car.
— Turn to the left (counter-clockwise). After the car has completed a 360-degree turn, turn right and straighten the car.
— Apply the brakes to stop the car gently.
— Return the gear selector to the Park position.

By now, you have made a good deal of progress in becoming a safe, skilful driver. If you have mastered the essential controls of your car, and can effortlessly perform the practice manoeuvres in the exercises above, you are ready for the next step — driving in actual traffic conditions. If you are relaxed and careful, it will be a pleasant experience — but don't forget to take your signed instruction permit!

5

lane control

In this section of the book we shall discuss the problems and situations you are likely to encounter on the public roads. The present chapter deals with the problems of sharing the road with other vehicles, of responding correctly to traffic signs, and of coping with the special problem of pedestrians. Your instructor will probably start you off on a quiet street where there will be a minimum of traffic. When he is confident that you have mastered this fundamental stage, you will be ready for the more complex situations which are covered in the following chapters.

In North America, we generally drive to the right and pass to the left, although certain exceptions, such as one-way streets, do exist. Unless you are intending to turn left within a short distance, you should drive in the right lane nearest the curb. In this position you will not hinder other traffic. Slow-moving traffic should always keep right.

TYPES OF LANES

Two-Lane Roads Without Markings

The diagram illustrates a two-lane road with no markings. On this type of road, you should mentally divide the road into two car widths. Remember you have to share the road with drivers of other vehicles as well as with pedestrians. If you are uncertain that there is enough space for two cars side by side, slow down and pull over to the side whenever another car approaches.

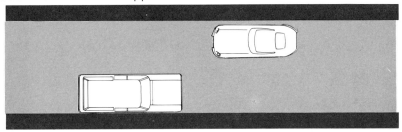

Two-Lane Roads With Centre Lines

The diagrams illustrate two-lane roads with centre markings. This type of road-marking is a great asset to the drivers, since it gives a clear guide to the space available for his automobile, and also indicates when it is safe to pass. Always keep in one lane only; *do not straddle the centre.*

Diagram A illustrates a broken centre line, which means either car may overtake and pass when the way is clear.

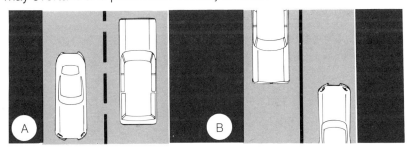

Diagram B illustrates a solid centre line, which indicates a division of the road into two equal parts. A driver should not cross the solid line to pass another vehicle unless the way ahead is clear. In some provinces, however, it is illegal to pass anything except a slow-moving vehicle.

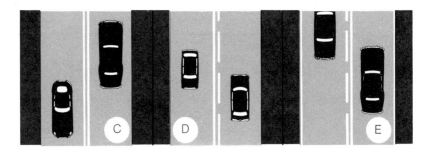

Diagram C illustrates two solid lines, which means neither car should pass.

Diagram D illustrates a solid line on the left and a broken centre line on the right. A driver on the right may pass a vehicle if the way is clear. However, a driver in the left lane should not pass.

Diagram E is the opposite to Diagram D.

Side Lines

The solid lines (in Diagram E) on the side of a road define the edge of the paved portion of a road.

Three-Lane Roads With Markings

The diagrams illustrate a three-lane road with markings. This road adds complications, because either driver can use the middle lane for passing or making a left-hand turn. On this type of road you should normally drive in the right lane and pass only when it is safe. *Do not straddle the lane markings*.

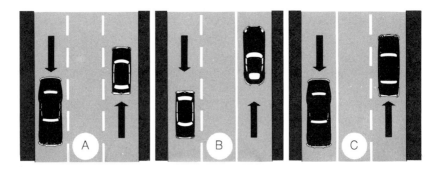

Four-Lane Highways With Markings

The diagram illustrates a typical four-lane road. Always keep well to the right, except when you intend to overtake and pass another vehicle or when you intend to make a left turn. Leave the right lane only when it is safe to do so.

If you are driving more slowly than other traffic, keep in the right-hand lane except when preparing for a left turn. At every opportunity do all you can to help faster traffic to go through. It is an offence to block overtaking traffic in the passing lane. Again, do not straddle the lane markings.

Four-Lane Highways With A Median

The diagram illustrates a typical four-lane road with a median. The same type of driving conditions apply with this type of road as with four lanes without a median. The median, in effect, separates the highway into two one-way roads, with several advantages: passing is easier; traffic congestion is reduced; glare from headlights is cut; and accidents are reduced, especially head-on collisions.

LANE CHANGING

Careful precautions should always be taken when changing lanes. Always be sure to check for other vehicles on the road. Your rear view mirrors, by their very name, imply that they show you the traffic conditions behind you. The side mirror suggests that it gives side vision. The most important thing to understand, however, is what the mirrors do **not** show you. These are the **blind spots** – the areas of vision that are obscured by your own car. These areas vary with different vehicles; every driver should be familiar with the blind spot of the car he is driving. Remember also to signal whenever you change lanes.

An excellent practice to adopt is a "lane-change drill," which will soon become one of the good habits that comprise safe driving. The sequence to follow is: (1) look in the mirrors to get a general picture of the following traffic; (2) signal; (3) "shoulder check" to the right or left; (4) maintain or increase speed during the lane-change, but under no circumstances slow down.

Overtaking And Passing

In North America, a vehicle overtaking a slower vehicle moving in the same direction generally passes on the left. Passing on the *right* is permitted:

1. When overtaking another vehicle making a left turn or signalling a left turn.
2. On one-way-traffic streets.
3. On streets and highways marked for multi-lanes.

Extreme care should be exercised in all the above situations, because other drivers may sometimes swerve to the right without warning. You must not drive off the roadway onto the shoulder to pass another vehicle.

How To Pass

More head-on collisions are caused by improper passing than by any other reason. It is extremely important, therefore, to know the rules for safe passing.

1. Look for signs and road-markings which will indicate whether or not it is safe to pass.
2. Pass another vehicle only when the way is clear ahead as well as behind.
3. Check your mirrors, and over your shoulder.
4. Signal, and sound your horn.
5. Pull out, accelerate, and proceed with caution.
6. Get well ahead of the other car, signal, and get back into the right lane.

Use extra care when passing in bad weather, at night, or under any other unfavourable conditions, because it is difficult to judge speed and distance.

If the vehicle you are passing speeds up, don't race. Turn back into line. Never overtake and pass another vehicle unless you **know** that you can do so without danger to yourself or to others who are approaching or overtaking you.

If you are being passed by another vehicle, never speed up but, if necessary, slow down to allow the other driver to pass you quickly, so that he can get back safely into the right lane ahead of you.

When Not To Pass

There are numerous occasions when it is dangerous to pass. Here are some of the most important situations where this rule applies.

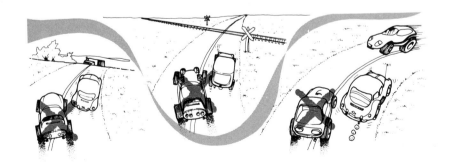

Do not drive to the left of the centre of a highway when approaching a curve or the crest of a hill; within a hundred feet of a bridge, viaduct, or tunnel where the driver's view is obstructed; or within a hundred feet of a level railway-crossing. These rules do not apply, however, to streets or highways on which one-way traffic only is permitted, or to highways divided into clearly-marked lanes where there are more such lanes for traffic in one direction than in the other direction.

IF IN DOUBT, DO NOT PASS!

Overtaking And Passing At Night

When approaching an oncoming vehicle at night, switch to the low beam of your headlights when you are at least 500 feet away. If the oncoming driver fails to dim *his* lights, watch the right-hand side of the road and keep well over to the right. Avoid looking into the glare of the lights of the oncoming vehicle. Do not switch your own headlights to high beam – two blinded drivers are more dangerous than one.

Use your low beam when following another vehicle within 200 feet except when in the act of overtaking and passing. Switch to high beam as you come alongside the vehicle you are overtaking. This applies on all highways including divided highways.

traffic signs and road markings

BASIC SHAPES EVERY DRIVER MUST KNOW

Vertical rectangle

White with black or other coloured lettering, these regulatory signs state the law, such as speed limits, parking regulations, and turning and passing movements.

Triangle

The yield right of way sign, yellow with black letters, means you must slow down at the intersection and stop if necessary. Cross traffic from either direction has the right of way.

Crossbuck

The crossbuck, the traditional symbol at highway-railway crossings, is white with the words ''Railway Crossing'' in black lettering. Watch for this sign and be prepared to stop.

Round

The railway crossing advance warning sign, yellow with a black crossbuck X, means a highway-railway crossing is ahead.

Diamond

The warning signs are yellow with black letters or symbols. They warn of dangerous or unusual conditions ahead, such as a curve, turn, dip, or side road.

Octagon

The stop sign, red with white lettering, means you must come to a full stop. Be sure the way is clear before proceeding through the intersection, and yield the right of way to approaching traffic.

Horizontal rectangle

With white letters on a green background, this sign indicates destination and information.

Pentagon

The school advance sign has a blue background and shows a white silhouette of a schoolboy and a schoolgirl. It warns that you are approaching a school zone. Slow down, drive with extra caution, and watch for children.

This new sign showing the speed limit in a school zone, is electrically illuminated only during the times of the day when children are in the area. Be alert and obey the maximum speed limit indicated on the sign.

Sign erected at places where children cross to and from school. Take extra care—watch for children.

Crossover sign

A crossover sign means you must yield the right of way to pedestrians in the crossover and allow them free and uninterrupted passage, slowing down or stopping if necessary. It is dangerous and unlawful to pass a vehicle within 100 feet of a pedestrian crossover.

hese signs indicate where you may or may not park or op.

Warns of traffic signal lights ahead. Slow down to enable you to stop if required by the lights.

This sign advises motorists to move over to the right as soon as it is safe to do so, since the left lane ends ahead.

Warns that you are entering a construction zone. Drive with caution and be prepared for changes in the speed limit.

This sign is erected on interchange ramps to indicate the safe speed of the ramp.

Indicates the angle that the railway tracks make with the roadway.

Reminds motorists that they must be prepared to share the road with on-coming traffic.

Traffic may travel in one direction only.

Sign is placed on traffic islands and requires you to pass to the right.

Warns of a low subway or underpass ahead. Overhead clearance will be as shown on the sign.

Signals that two lanes of traffic are joining into one. Drivers in both lanes are equally responsible for smooth merging of traffic.

Lane 1

Lane 2

Lane 3

These signs are mounted above the roadway on the approach to an intersection and each sign is centred over the lane it controls. When in a lane controlled by one of these signs, the motorist must only make the manoeuvre indicated on the sign. A driver in lane 1 must turn left. Lane 2 is optional, either left or straight ahead. Lane 3 must turn right.

ymbol traffic signs, conforming to international standards, have been adopted in many areas. A new sign will be used hen an old sign needs replacing. Since the transition from old to new signs is expected to extend over some years, rivers must be familiar with both the old and the new signs.

OLD	NEW

hen pavement is slippery or wet, reduce speed, do not ake violently or change direction suddenly. Increase the stance between your car and the one ahead.

OLD	NEW

The pavement ahead is not as wide as the pavement on which you are driving.

OLD	NEW

arns of a steep hill ahead. Slow down, shift to lower ear (or gear range in cars with automatic transmission). ngage low gear if the hill is very steep.

OLD	NEW

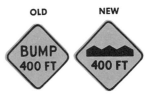

Warns of a bump or uneven spot on the pavement or road. Reduce speed and maintain alert control of your vehicle when going over the bump.

OLD	NEW

arns of a railway crossing ahead. Be on the alert for proaching trains.

OLD	NEW

Warns that the bridge ahead has a road width of 16' to 20' and has two lanes. Also indicates a bridge narrower than the approaching pavement. Take care; drive slowly.

OLD	NEW

dicates that the highway ahead is split into two separate adways by a median or boulevard. Keep to the right-nd roadway. Each roadway carries one-way traffic.

OLD	NEW

Indicates that the highway ahead becomes a single road-way with traffic in both directions on the same roadway. Keep to the right half of the roadway.

OLD   NEW

You must not enter this street when confronted by this sign.

OLD   NEW

You must not make a left turn at this intersection.

OLD   NEW

This sign warns of a change in maximum speed ahead.

OLD   NEW

This sign shows that the maximum speed permitted under ideal conditions is 30 miles per hour.

OLD   NEW

You must not turn your vehicle around in the roadway to travel in the opposite direction.

OLD   NEW

No heavy trucks are allowed on a street or highway where this sign is posted.

OLD   NEW

Warns of a stop sign ahead. Slow down to enable you to stop safely.

OLD   NEW

This sign warns that there are men working ahead.

More Traffic Signs and What They Mean

This sign shows direction to a city, town, or village.

You are coming to the junction of two King's Highways.

This sign warns of a slow moving vehicle ahead. Slow moving vehicle signs are required to be attached to the rear of any farm tractor or self-propelled implement of husbandry or any vehicle towed by either of them when operated on a highway, except when crossing a highway.

Trucks may use a street or highway where this sign is posted.

Motorized snow vehicles are prohibited on a street or highway where this sign is posted.

Motorized snow vehicles are permitted on a street or highway where this sign is posted.

This sign warns of a slight bend or curve in the road ahead.

This sign warns of a road branching off from a travelled route.

This sign warns of a winding road ahead.

Warns that the bridge ahead may have a road width of 18' or less. Give right of way to the first vehicle to arrive at the bridge.

This sign warns of a hidden road crossing the travelled route at right angles.

This sign warns of a right turn followed by a left turn or bend in the road ahead.

Warns of a sharp turn or bend in road in the direction shown by the arrow. The checkerboard border is a warning of danger. Slow down; exercise added care.

This sign warns of a sharp bend or turn in the road ahead.

Warns that the road ahead is not as wide as the road you are on and may not be wide enough for two vehicles side by side.

SIGNAL LIGHTS

Green

A green signal-light means you may proceed if the way is clear. Yield the right-of-way to any vehicles and pedestrians who were still in the intersection when the light changed.

When making a turn on a green signal-light, remember that pedestrians crossing on the green light have the right-of-way.

Flashing Green

Where a flashing green light is used, vehicles facing that light may turn left, turn right, or go through, while opposing traffic faces a red light. In some localities, a green arrow is used instead of a flashing green; in this situation, of course, drivers may proceed only in the direction of the arrow. See page 60.

Amber

An amber signal-light indicates that the red signal is about to appear. You must come to a full stop unless such a stop cannot be made in safety. If it is not safe to stop, proceed with extreme caution. The period that the amber light is on allows time to clear the intersection before cross-traffic begins to flow.

Red

A red signal-light indicates that you must come to a complete stop. In some provinces, you may proceed with a right turn after having stopped, providing the right-of-way is given to pedestrians and other traffic in the intersection. In other provinces, however, a right turn is not allowed on a red light.

Red With A Green Arrow

When a red signal-light and a green arrow are shown together, you may enter the intersection, but only to move in the direction shown by the arrow. It is not necessary to stop, but you should slow down, drive very carefully, and yield the right-of-way to pedestrians and other traffic using the intersection.

Flashing Amber

A flashing amber light means you must slow down and proceed with caution. This light may be situated overhead, or may be part of a standard traffic-control light.

Flashing Red

A flashing red light means you must bring your vehicle to a stop and proceed only when it is safe to do so. Like the flashing amber, the flashing red light may be overhead or part of a standard traffic-control signal light.

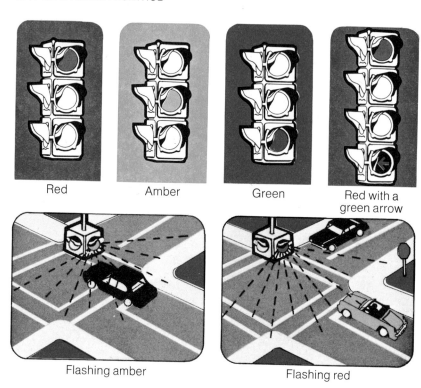

| Red | Amber | Green | Red with a green arrow |

Flashing amber   Flashing red

The sequence in which the lights change is:

Red to Green
Green to Amber
Amber to Red

Some lights are hung horizontally, but the sequence remains the same.

INTERSECTION PAVEMENT MARKINGS

Hash marks or diagonal stripes are painted on the pavement at the approach to some major intersections. These indicate an exclusive lane for left- or right-turning vehicles. Once in the turning lane, the motorist must turn left or right only, as the case may be.

Pavement arrows are used to show the direction in which the driver must move when using the lane concerned. In some cases the words **Right-Turn Lane** or **Left-Turn Lane** are included with the arrows as an additional guide.

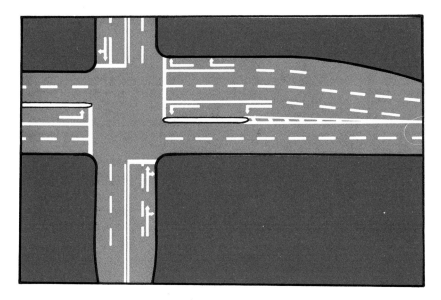

Right-Of-Way At Intersections

When approaching an intersection unmarked by signal lights, stop signs, or yield signs at the same time as another vehicle — yield the right-of-way to the vehicle approaching from the right.

A stop sign means that you must bring your vehicle to a full stop before entering the intersection. Before proceeding, give way to pedestrians and to vehicles approaching the intersection so closely that it is hazardous. If in doubt, give way. The driver approaching on the other highway must yield the right-of-way to vehicles lawfully in the intersection.

At intersections where stop signs are located at all four corners, the first car to come to a complete stop should be given the right-of-way.

You should always yield the right-of-way to a pedestrian.

The driver of a vehicle that is turning should yield the right-of-way to all oncoming traffic.

A vehicle emerging from a driveway shall yield the right-of-way to oncoming traffic and pedestrians.

DRIVING ALONG

Flying an airplane has been described as 99 per cent boredom and 1 per cent sheer terror. One would hope that this is not true; at any rate, such a description should never apply to driving a car. It is all too easy, in the course of routine driving, for alertness and concentration to slacken even momentarily. Remember that a fraction of a second is all that it takes to cause death or a lifetime of suffering; remember this particularly when you are in a hurry. In one second, when travelling at 30 miles per hour, your car travels 44 feet. Concentrate on the job of driving. When possible, keep pace with the general traffic-stream but obey speed limits. This eliminates much of the unnecessary overtaking, passing, and chance-taking that can lead to a collision.

Check On Traffic

Don't turn around to talk or view the scenery. When you are watching traffic behind, frequent quick glances are better than one long look. It is unwise to assume that pedestrians or other drivers will always take the correct and proper action.

Glance in your mirrors before you change traffic lanes, overtake, stop, turn, or start away from a parked position. Know what's behind you at all times by quick glances in the mirrors – and don't forget to allow for the blind spot. Turning your head to check is a further safety precaution.

If A Tire Blows . . .

Don't jam on the brakes. Let up on the accelerator and concentrate on steering. If you suddenly apply the brakes when a rear tire blows, a tailsway is set up that is difficult to control, and your car may overturn. Whether the front or rear tire blows, skilful steering is most important.

Emergency Vehicles

If you hear the siren or bell of a police car, fire truck, ambulance, or public utility emergency vehicle; or see a flashing red light mounted on the vehicle, get out of the way. Bring your car to a stop as near as possible to the side of the road. Do not block an intersection.

In some provinces, volunteer fire-fighters are authorized to display an amber and white flashing light showing the letters "V.F.F." on their vehicles when proceeding to a fire or other emergency. Give such vehicles the right-of-way.

Fixed Objects In The Road

Two solid lines enclosing diagonal markings (as shown in the diagram) are painted on the pavement at the approach to a fixed object in or near the roadway, such as a divided underpass, bridge pier, concrete island, or other such hazard. In addition, yellow and black markings are painted on the fixed objects themselves to ensure adequate advance warning of the hazards ahead.

If A Wheel Runs Off The Pavement . . .

If a wheel runs onto a soft or depressed shoulder, grip the steering wheel firmly to maintain course. Don't try to get the car back on the road by jerking the wheel. Before trying to steer back onto the pavement, reduce speed and continue with the wheels on the shoulder. Steer on to the pavement as soon as traffic permits.

Opening Doors And Impeding Traffic

Always be careful when opening the door on the traffic-side of the car. In some provinces, it is an offence: (1) to open the door of a motor vehicle without making sure that such action will not interfere with the movement of or endanger any other person or vehicle; or (2) to leave a door next to traffic open longer than necessary to load or unload passengers.

Buses

A driver approaching a stopped bus should always proceed with caution, and be ready for the unexpected. There is always the chance that passengers who are leaving the bus may decide to walk in front before the bus leaves the stop. Others may run in front of the motorist, trying to catch the bus before it pulls away.

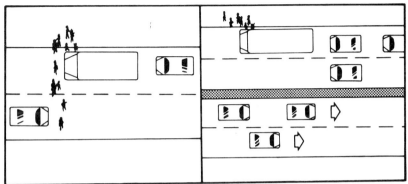

TWO LANE HIGHWAY   **FOUR LANE HIGHWAY WITH MEDIAN STRIP**

OVERTAKING OR MEETING SCHOOL BUSES

Particular care is necessary in traffic situations involving school buses. If a stationary school bus is flashing its red signal-lights, children are entering or leaving, or else preparing to do so. Traffic heading in either direction must stop before reaching the bus. Cars may not proceed until the bus resumes motion or until its signal lights are turned off. The only exception to this rule is that cars are not required to stop if a median strip separates their lane from the lane in which the bus is waiting. Even in this situation, it is still a good idea to drive with extra caution — there is just no way of predicting what children will do.

Slow Driving

For reasons of courtesy and consideration as well as safety, no one should drive at such a slow rate of speed as to block the normal and reasonable movement of traffic on the highways. Slow-moving vehicles, such as farm tractors, are required to carry a "slow-moving vehicle" sign at the rear.

Streetcars

Always pass streetcars on the right-hand side. (Passing on the left is permitted on one-way streets.) If the streetcar is stopped to pick up or discharge passengers, stay at least six feet behind the rear door at which passengers are getting on or off. This rule does not apply at a properly-designated safety island or zone.

Safety Zone

Pass safety islands and zones at a reasonable speed. Always make allowance for sudden or unexpected pedestrian actions.

When Following Other Vehicles — Keep Your Distance

Following too closely is one of the most hazardous driver actions, and is a violation of the law. The driver behind is usually responsible for rear-end collisions. When traffic speed increases, increase the distance between your car and the one ahead accordingly.

Good drivers allow at least one car length for each 10 miles per hour of car speed. For example, when driving at 50, stay at least 5 car-lengths to the rear; at 30, leave at least 3 car lengths.

When To Reduce Speed

Slow down at all crossings, street intersections, schools, and when passing parked cars. Slow down when driving under adverse conditions such as rain, snow, or fog. A good driver will always drive according to conditions.

Reverse Traffic-Flow

Some large cities use a "reverse traffic-flow" system. The purpose of this is to ease the congested traffic in the city. A motorist who is entering a city in the morning may find he is on a one-way street between certain hours. In the evening, however, the same street may be one-way in the opposite direction! Be very careful of this in unfamiliar cities.

Electric Traffic-Controls

An electronic overhead traffic-control system is a device to measure the density of traffic, and, using a computer, calculate the best speed to maintain a smooth flow of cars at that point. The calculated speed limit appears on an overhead signal board, and may vary constantly as conditions change. This type of system has helped to ease the congestion of traffic on busy roads.

Controlled Pedestrian Crossings

At intersections, always allow pedestrians time to get clear of the crossing before moving ahead on the "GO" signal. Even if you feel that you have the right-of-way, always let the pedestrian go first.

UNCONTROLLED PEDESTRIAN CROSSINGS

At this type of a crossing, a driver must use the utmost care when approaching the intersection. Sometimes there are no painted lines on the road to indicate the pedestrian crossing; particular care is needed in these cases, since pedestrians may tend to wander somewhat haphazardly, rather than proceed straight across. In effect, therefore, the intersection begins at the edges of the sidewalk.

PEDESTRIAN CROSSWALKS

At pedestrian crosswalks, a driver must yield the right-of-way to any pedestrians in the crosswalk and allow them free and uninterrupted passage, slowing down or stopping if necessary.

It is dangerous and may be unlawful to pass a vehicle within 100 feet of a pedestrian crosswalk.

Crosswalks are identified by signs and markings as shown in this photo. Remember, crosswalks are often located some distance from an intersection.

In the normal course of driving it is probable that you will eventually encounter most of the situations touched upon in this chapter, and probably many other situations as well. This is no cause for concern. If you take reasonable precautions and always use common sense, you may count on endless miles of problem-free motoring.

6

making turns in traffic

In the previous chapter we discussed some of the situations you might encounter while driving in traffic. In this chapter, we shall concentrate on one particular traffic situation: the problem of making turns.

TURNING PROCEDURES

Many collisions are caused by drivers who, either through ignorance or negligence, fail to make right or left turns correctly. There are certain steps which all drivers should take before making turns:

1. Decide on the place you intend to turn before you reach it. It is dangerous to decide at the last second to make a turn.
2. Check your mirrors and your blind spot for other vehicles before you change lanes.
3. You should give a signal well ahead of your turning point in order to give ample warning to others. If using a hand-signal, hold it until you are close enough to the intersection so that pedestrians and other drivers are aware of your intention to turn. Do not hold the hand-signal while making your turn, however; you need both hands on the wheel.

4. Move into the proper lane as soon as possible. The faster the traffic is moving, the sooner you should get into the proper lane for your turn.

5. Make turns at low speed, keeping your car under complete control.

6. Make your turn as soon as traffic conditions permit. Do not keep the traffic behind you waiting unnecessarily.

7. If you are stopped in an intersection to make a left turn, and waiting for approaching traffic to clear, do not turn the steering wheel to the left until you are sure you can complete the turn. With the wheels turned to the left, your car could be pushed into the path of approaching traffic if struck from the rear.

8. Make your turns correctly as shown in the following pages. This will be easy if you are in the proper lane and proceeding slowly enough at the time you begin to turn.

9. Complete your turn into the proper lane.

Right Turn Approach

Before making a right turn, the automobile should be in the right-hand lane and parallel to the curb. The distance from the curb to the side of the automobile should be three feet. At this point your speed should be less than 10 miles per hour. If you are driving a manual-transmission car, you should be in second gear.

Well before you reach the intersection, signal your turn and move to the right-hand lane when the way is clear. Look ahead, and to the left and right, before starting to make your turn. Keep your car three feet from the curb as you make the turn. Watch for pedestrians, who have the right-of-way.

As the car slowly rolls out across the crosswalk lines, you must judge when to begin the right turn. This is the most difficult part of the turn. Each corner is slightly different; you must assess the degree of sharpness and turn accordingly. A good general rule is, begin turning hand-over-hand as the front wheels reach the point where the curb turns. If you start too soon, the rear wheels will strike or climb the curb. If you start turning too late, the car will swing wide and be in the wrong lane as you complete the turn.

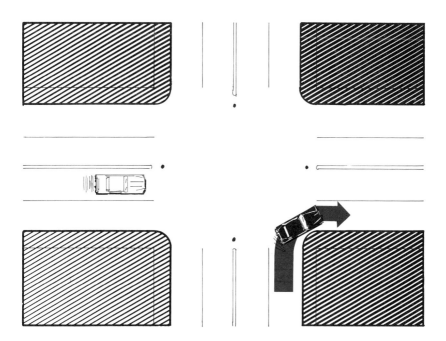

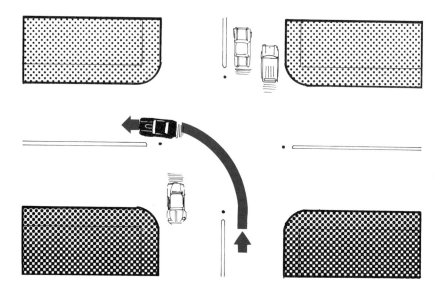

Left Turn Approach

The law states that in order to make a left turn, the driver must begin from the "most left" legal position on the roadway. In some cases it is necessary to make a lane change before turning left.

Mirror check, shoulder check, signal left and, if the way is clear, enter the proper lane. Watch for pedestrians.

Well before you reach the intersection, slow down to less than 10 miles per hour and *again* signal your intention to turn left. Look behind for traffic and move as close to the centre line as possible (that is, the line separating your lane from the nearest lane of oncoming traffic). Look ahead to the left and right before starting to make the turn. Wait until all oncoming traffic is clear of the intersection. Cars making a left-hand turn **must** surrender the right-of-way to oncoming traffic going straight through the intersection.

In some cities, left turns are simplified by curving yellow lines on the road, which act as guides. Where these do not exist, enter the intersection to the right of the centre point (as shown). Leave the intersection by passing to the right of, and as close as practicable to, the centre line of the highway being entered.

When you are heading straight again, accelerate gently to regain speed. Be careful if you accelerate while you are still turning — the car may skid, causing you to lose control.

Making Left Turns At Traffic Signals

In busy areas of the city, traffic signals are essential to keep traffic moving smoothly. If you are making a left turn, however, traffic signals in one sense pose an additional problem: that of a "time limit" to how long you can wait for oncoming traffic. Once you have entered the intersection on a green light, complete your turn at the first safe opportunity. If the light turns amber or red, you must still turn when the way is clear. This manoeuvre is legal, and it is better to turn than to block the intersection.

ADVANCED GREEN FLASHING LIGHT

In North America, the flashing green light is a standard method of making left-hand turns at intersections both easier and safer.

The flashing green appears at the beginning of the "light cycle," immediately following the red light. If you are turning right or proceeding straight through the intersection, the flashing green is treated exactly the same as a regular green signal. If you are turning left, however, you will have a "protected turn." This has two important benefits:

1. There should be no oncoming traffic in the intersection, since these vehicles will still be facing a red light.
2. There should be no pedestrians in your path, since a "Don't Walk" signal will be on.

The duration of the flashing light is variable; that is, some intersections have flashing green signals with a longer duration than others. In fact, the duration of the flashing green may change at the same intersection during different parts of the day. Or, there may be a flashing green at one time of day and only a regular green at others. Always keep these potential variations in mind.

When a flashing green ends, the steady green will begin, so that oncoming vehicles will be crossing the intersection. This traffic has the right-of-way, and must be allowed to proceed before you make your turn. If you get caught in the intersection, do not panic; stop and wait for a break in the traffic, and then complete your turn. If there is no break in the traffic, complete your turn when the light turns amber.

At some intersections, you will see a green arrow appear. You may enter the intersection to move only in the direction shown by the arrow.

EXTENDED FLASHING GREEN

The extended flashing green, although not quite as common as the advanced green, offers a similar advantage to left-turning traffic. The extended flashing green, as the name implies, comes after the regular green and before the amber. While the flashing green is on, all pedestrians and oncoming traffic are stopped. Thus a flashing green, whether extended or advanced, still gives a protected left turn to the driver.

Making a Left Turn From A Two-Lane Street
Into Another Two-Lane Street

As you near the corner, your speed should be less than 10 miles per hour. It is important to judge how sharply to turn your car. If you turn too late you will go too wide, so that you may run up on the sidewalk or shoulder. If you turn too soon, you may end up in the opposing lane. Therefore, you should turn the steering wheel before the front of the car reaches the centre of the intersection. Once you have completed the turn, resume speed once again.

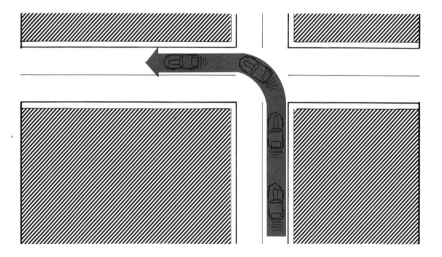

Making A Left Turn From A Two-Lane
Street Into A Divided Four-Lane Street

Turning from a normal two-way road onto a divided highway can be very confusing. The wide expanse of the big road could cause the

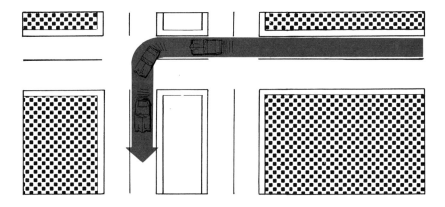

driver to panic and turn up the wrong side of the divider strip or median. Take your time; as you move forward, watch for oncoming cars and pedestrians, and complete your turn into the lane, just to the right of the median. Always be careful to stay completely in your lane, clear the corner, speed up, and lane-change to the right when traffic is clear (see illustration).

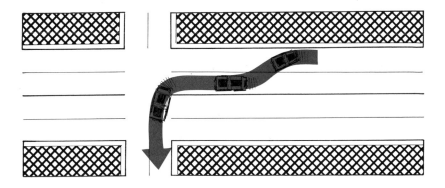

Making A Left Turn From A Two-Way Street Into A One-Way Street

When turning into a one-way street, you must by law complete your turn as far to the left as possible. Well back from the intersection, signal your intention to turn left. Look behind for traffic, then move as close to the centre line as possible when the way is clear. Look ahead and to the left and right before starting to make your turn.

Begin the turn from just to the right of the point (as shown) where the centre line meets the intersecting street. When the turn is completed, resume speed, mirror check, shoulder check, signal, and then change to the right lane.

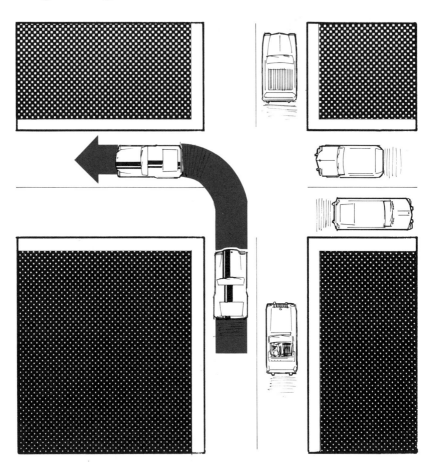

Making A Left Turn From A One-Way Street Into A Two-Lane Street

Well before the intersection, signal your intention to turn left. Move to the left side of the one-way street when the way is clear.

Look ahead, to the left, and to the right, before starting to make your turn.

Make your turn to the right of, and as close as practicable to, the centre line.

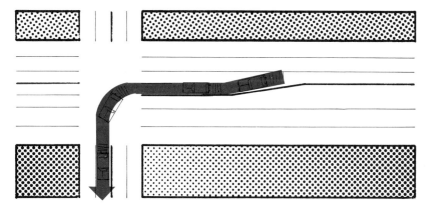

*Making A Left Turn From A Multiple Lane Street
(More Than Four Lanes) Into A Four-Lane Street*

Well before the intersection, mirror check and shoulder check, signal left, and if the way is clear, move into the proper lane. Signal your intention that you are going to make a left turn. In some cities and towns, both inner lanes may be allowed to make a left turn. As always, be alert.

Using Traffic Circles

The arrows of the diagram indicate the path your car should follow. The safest way to travel in a traffic circle is to know before you enter what lane you must use. Crossing lanes in a traffic circle could result in a serious accident because of the blind spots in the rear of your automobile.

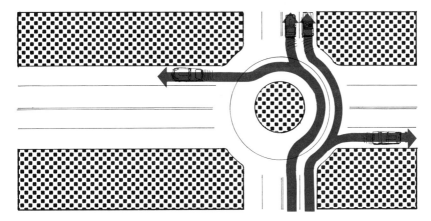

Turning About Or "Three-Point" Turn

At times it is necessary to turn your car in close quarters. To turn about, start from the extreme right side, check for other traffic, give the proper turn signal, and when the way is clear, turn the steering wheel sharply to the left while inching forward.

When you have turned the wheels completely to the left, drive slowly forward to within a few inches of the left curb or edge of the roadway. Just before stopping, turn the wheels quickly to the right. After stopping, put the gear selector in Reverse and back slowly to within a few inches of the curb. Just before stopping, turn the wheels quickly to the left.

Repeat these manoeuvres until you have completed your turn.

Turning around is not permitted on many streets where the turn may be hazardous or may delay traffic. Often the simplest and best method is just to drive around the block.

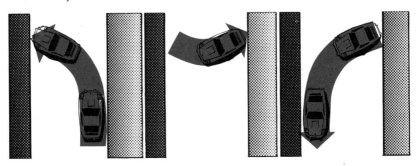

Turning About At An Intersection

This type of turn is made where there is light traffic, and good visibility prevails. The procedure is as follows:

1. Signal your stop.
2. Check all traffic.
3. Drive past the intersection.
4. Stop.
5. Backing up, turn into the side street. Stop when the front bumper of the car is just past the cross-walk.
6. Signal your turn.
7. Check for traffic and pedestrians.
8. Driving forward, complete your turn.

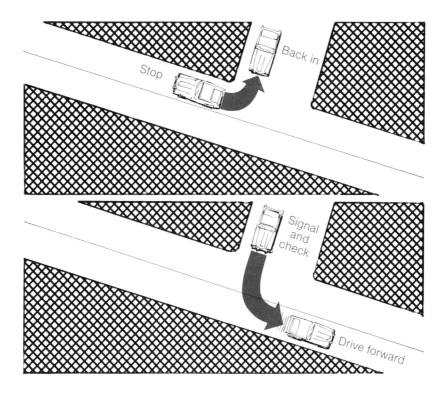

Making "U-Turns"

A "U-turn" is made by turning a car around to the opposite direction in one complete motion. Never make a U-turn in an intersection, near a curve, or at the crest of a hill — you could be caught by oncoming traffic. Many localities do not allow U-turns: if in doubt, drive around the block or turn at a safe intersection.

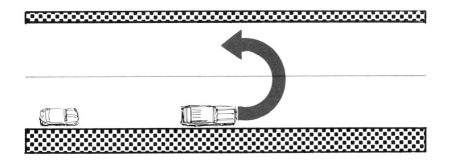

Procedure for U-turns:
1. Stop near the right-hand curb (within six inches).
2. Check for all traffic.
3. Check the blind spots.
4. Signal for a left turn.
5. Moving slowly forward, turn the steering wheel rapidly (hand-over-hand method).
6. When the turn is completed, proceed in the proper lane.

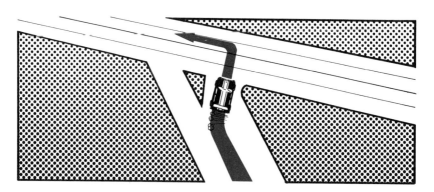

Turning At A "Y" Intersection

A right turn at this intersection is the same as any other right turn. However, when you are going to make a *left* turn, you should first swing to the right and stop at a right angle to the traffic on the through road (see illustration). When the car is in this position you will have a clear view of the intersection; you will also be stopped in a position where other drivers can see you and the car.

Mirror check, shoulder check, signal left, and if the way is clear, make your left turn properly.

Obstacles And Special Problems In Turning

PEDESTRIANS

The problem of pedestrians at intersections was discussed in the previous chapter. When you are *turning* at the intersection, however, the problem becomes greater still. As you approach the turn, slow down, look to the corner, and try to guess what the pedestrian might do. Always put yourself in a pedestrian's place: what will he do as you reach the turn? He may even walk right in front of you, so slow down, and be prepared to stop. If you expect the worst you will never be surprised when a pedestrian steps out. The most dangerous pedestrian of all is the one walking off the near corner; he has his back to you and is within three feet of your right fender — so watch out. Always remember, pedestrians have the right-of-way.

PARKED CARS

Parked cars will always be a hazard on right turns. A good driver will anticipate this problem by watching for parked cars close to the corner. It may be necessary to leave the right lane, pass the parked car, and then come back to the right lane to make the turn. Sometimes it is even necessary to make a right turn from the centre lane if a car is illegally parked too close to the corner.

TRUCKS AND BUSES

Some large vehicles, because of their size, cannot make proper right turns. A truck driver, for instance, may have to begin a right turn from the outside lane and complete his turn in the outside lane again — not because of carelessness, but because of sheer necessity. Bus drivers have similar problems. Always watch the signals on a bus or truck so as not to be taken by surprise.

As with the previous chapter, this chapter has indicated a number of situations that you are likely to encounter at some stage of your driving career. As with driving in the lanes, turning should present no special problem. The same advice still applies — be alert, exercise caution, and always use your common sense.

7

parking

A skilled driver is able to park his vehicle with ease in any parking space. Depending on the type of space provided, there are two techniques that can be used: parallel parking and angle parking. Here are the steps in parking your vehicle parallel to the curb.

PARALLEL PARKING

1. Approach the parking space with your car between one and one-half and two feet to the left of the parked cars on your right.
2. Check traffic and give the proper signal for stopping.
3. Stop your vehicle beside the car in front of the space you will be using. Be sure your car is one and one-half to two feet from this vehicle, and have your rear bumper in line with the rear bumper of the other car.
4. After shifting to Reverse, check oncoming traffic, and look over your right shoulder. Back slowly, turning your steering wheel rapidly to your right until you are at a 45 degree angle to the curb. Straighten your wheels and continue backing.

5. Continue this path (45 degrees) until the front bumper of your car is opposite the rear bumper of the car you are parking behind.
6. Turn your wheel sharply to the left while continuing to back slowly into the parking space.
7. Be sure you are watching the gap between your car and the vehicle behind you. Do not hit the car behind.
8. Move the car slowly forward, straightening the wheels as you go. Stop when your car is equally-spaced between the car in front and the car behind. There should be no more than nine inches between your right door and the curb.
9. Set the parking brake. Place the selector lever in the Park position. Remove the key and lock the doors.

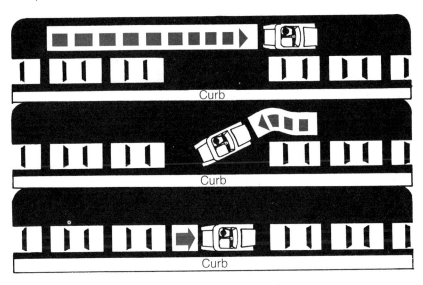

Once you have parked your car, the next procedure you must know is how to move your car out of the parking space and into the driving lane.

1. Keep your wheels straight, and back up until your rear bumper is almost touching the car behind.
2. Stop. Shift the selector to the Drive position.
3. Check oncoming traffic.
4. Signal for a left turn. In a line of parked cars, use your left arm for the signal to make sure you will be seen.

5. When the way is clear, start moving slowly forward, turning the steering wheel rapidly to the left.

6. When the front half of your car is in the right-hand traffic lane, begin turning the steering wheel to your right. Check repeatedly to see that the right side of your car bumper does not strike the car in front of the parking space.

Many beginning drivers are worried by the above manoeuvre. Be sure you understand the above steps, and practise until you are competent in parallel parking.

ANGLE PARKING

Angle parking is another skill which all drivers must know. Carefully note the diagrams and the steps to make sure you know where and when to turn to fit your car into an angle parking-space.

1. Check traffic and give the proper signal.

2. Approach the parking space with your car about five feet from the parked cars on your right.

3. When the front bumper is in line with the parking-space entrance, begin steering to your right.

4. Move slowly and steer carefully to be sure that the left edge of your front bumper does not strike the car to the left of the space, and the right side of your car does not strike the car on your right.

5. Watch the front end of your car, and be sure that your bumper is *close* to any barrier but not touching it. If there is a curb, ease your wheels close to it.

6. Set the parking brake.

7. Place the gear selector in the Park position.

Leaving an angle parking-space is perhaps more hazardous than entering, because of the blind areas created by the cars to your right. Here is the recommended procedure to follow:

1. Shift to Reverse. Check for traffic and pedestrians. Check blind spots.
2. Moving slowly and cautiously, inch the car backwards until you can be absolutely sure that the traffic is clear. Stop if a car is approaching.
3. When traffic permits, proceed straight back. As your front bumper passes the rear bumper of the car on your left, steer sharply to your right.
4. When your car is parallel to the edge of the street or roadway, stop, shift to forward gear, and proceed.

PARKING ON A HILL

Have you ever watched a car roll downhill with no driver? Your first instinct might be to laugh, but the realization of how dangerous it is soon follows. To avoid such a situation for your car, follow the next three rules carefully.

1. When you are parking uphill on a street with a curb, the front wheels should be pointed to the left. Put the gear selector in Park, and set the parking brake.
2. When you are parking downhill on a street with a curb, the front wheels should be pointed to the right. Put the gear selector in Park, and set the parking brake.
3. When you are parking uphill or downhill on a roadway which does not have a curb, the front wheels should be pointed to the right. Put the gear selector in Park, and set the parking brake.

Facing uphill with curb
Turn wheels from curb

Facing downhill with curb
Turn wheels to curb

Facing up or downhill without curb
Turn wheels to right

8

highway driving

Highway engineering and construction have made great advances in the past 30 years. While existing highways are being improved, multi-lane super-highways are being designed and built, making it possible to increase speed limits. These road systems can be divided into three main types:

1. The multi-lane, controlled-access highway, or freeway. Driving techniques for this type of highway are discussed in Chapter 9.
2. Class A highways, which have the following characteristics:
   – Driving lanes with a minimum width of 12 feet.
   – Wide, well-graded shoulders.
   – High-speed banked curves.
   – Easy grades with dual uphill lanes for passing slow-moving vehicles.
   – Constant maintenance during winter driving conditions (sanding, ploughing, etc.).
3. Secondary road systems, having the following characteristics:
   – Narrow driving lanes.
   – Narrow graded shoulders.
   – Sharper curves.
   – Steeper grades.
   – Slower posted speeds.

Modern highways, coupled with the introduction of more powerful cars, have made higher average speeds possible for motor vehicles.

This need for increased average speed seems to have overshadowed the need for improvements in safety; statistics show that in spite of all the modern engineering techniques on highways and vehicles, there are approximately three times as many fatal accidents on our highways as there are on our urban streets where speeds are much lower.

Why this is so is a complex question, but it is a safe bet that highway design and automobile deficiencies are the least influential factors, although they most certainly do play some part. Increased speed and all of its effects, on the other hand, are probably the biggest contributing factor. Therefore, in the following section we shall discuss the significance and effect of speed, from the point of view of the laws of physics that govern the behaviour of moving vehicles.

THE LAWS OF PHYSICS AND THEIR EFFECT ON DRIVING

Increased speed makes the laws of physics become more and more important to the driver. These laws, although not enforced by a policeman or written by a law-producing body, are absolutely binding on all drivers, and no one can relax their effect.

The laws of physics control any and every object that moves. The particular laws which apply to driving cover areas such as friction, centrifugal force and inertia, impact, and gravity. You should always remember that these laws apply to city driving as well as to driving on the highway, because their significance increases proportionately with the speed at which you are travelling. However, this chapter on highway driving would seem the best place to discuss their importance.

Proper sight requires sufficient light *and* time for a picture to impose itself on the retina of the eye, be relayed to the brain, and thereby trigger a reaction by the driver. This means that traffic signs, signals, and pavement markings become increasingly important when driving at higher speeds. These give the driver advance warning of any curves, hills, intersections, or railway crossings that may be ahead, as well as intended manoeuvres by other drivers. A driver must learn to recognize all signs and signals instantly, for at higher speeds the time for recognition and reaction becomes shorter and shorter. To facilitate recognition, signs and signals throughout Canada are generally standardized by shape and colour; many are "reflectorized" or lighted so they can be seen easily even at night. Remember — it takes time to observe a sign, signal, or condition, and then react to it. Reaction time for a given driver is fairly constant, but the distance travelled in this time is directly related to speed. Therefore, stopping distances and distances required for evasive action become greater as speed is increased.

Friction

Friction is the force which opposes the motion of one surface over another, and is the means through which a vehicle may move in a straight line, or may turn or stop. This force is exerted entirely through four small friction-areas as shown at right — the tires.

The graph shows stopping distances under ideal conditions (using an average reaction time of .75 seconds). These conditions

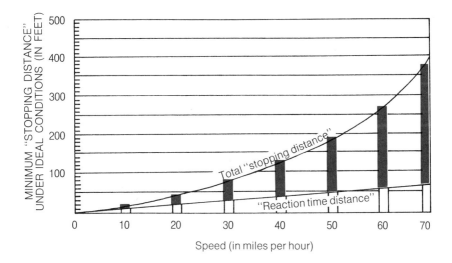

only occur part of the time, however: should the force of friction be reduced by ice, snow, rain, oil, mud, loose gravel, rough surface, or poor tires, then stopping distances will increase drastically and evasive manoeuvres will become much more difficult, or even impossible.

Because stopping distance increases more rapidly than speed, it is important to allow a greater distance between your car and the car in front as your speed increases. The following chart illustrates the absolute necessity of leaving at least one car length for each ten miles per hour that you are travelling between you and the car ahead.

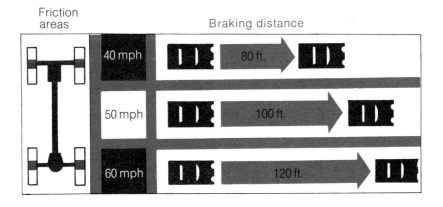

Inertia And Centrifugal Force

If at any time the frictional force, or "traction," between the four small tire-areas and the road surface is lost, control is lost as well, and one or both of the following physical forces may determine the situation: **inertia**, the tendency of a moving body to keep moving in a straight line unless an outside force acts to change its direction of motion; and **centrifugal force**, the tendency of a moving body turning about a centre to fly away from that centre. Centrifugal force can be demonstrated by placing a weight on the end of a string and swinging it in a circular motion. If the string is released or breaks, the weight will leave the circular path and continue in a straight line.

Obviously, a similar effect can happen to a turning vehicle. A car driving around a curve must overcome the centrifugal force in order to make the turn. If the centrifugal force is greater than the friction between the tires and the road, the car will not be able to turn, but will skid off the highway. The key point is that the friction increases with speed, but the centrifugal force increases even more rapidly. Therefore, the faster your speed, or the sharper the turn, the greater is the chance that you will be unable to get around safely. If you remember this principle, you will realize that you must slow down before entering a curve, especially if the road is slightly slippery.

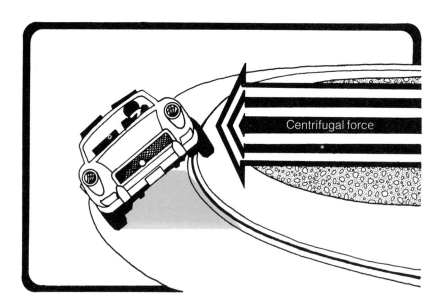

Centrifugal force

Brakes should never be applied after entering a curve, as this has a tendency to reduce the friction between the wheels and the road. Remember, friction enables you to move your car, control it, and stop it. When you consider that for each tire the area touching the road surface is about equal to the size of your hand, it is understandable that many factors can cause loss of friction, and resultant loss of control. The greater the speed, the greater the possibility this may happen — and the greater the consequences. Speed must always be adjusted to suit road conditions.

As well as the speed of the car, another factor determining whether or not you will be able to make a turn safely is the angle at which the road is "banked" through the curve. There are three basic types of curves. The easiest is a banked turn (similar to a race track); the second, a flat road surface; and the third, a crowned surface. The flat road surface is dangerous at high speed, and in comparison, in a turn, the crowned surface can only be negotiated at low speeds because the car is tilted against the direction of the curve. On entering sharp curves, there is usually an advisory speed sign posted, telling you the speed at which the curve may be safely taken. One who ignores these signs is indeed a very foolish driver.

Kinetic Energy And The Force Of Impact

If control of a car is lost, the usual result is collision, either with another car or with a fixed object. The all-important variable in this situation is the **force of impact**.

The force of impact itself is a function of the speed and the weight of the car. If you double the speed of a car before collision, the force of impact is *four times* as great. If you triple the speed of the car, the force of impact is multiplied *nine times*! Weight also has a part to play here; if the weight of the vehicle doubles, the force of impact doubles too. The total result of doubling the speed and the weight of the vehicle would be to increase the force of impact eight times. Therefore, any collision would necessarily be eight times as damaging. In effect, the impact of hitting a solid object at 30 miles per hour is like driving off a three-story building.

Highway engineers use several techniques to reduce the force of impact in cases of unavoidable contact with surrounding objects. Smooth metal guard-rails allow a car to glance off rather than hit

Force of impact

solidly. Wide road-shoulders, free of obstacles such as trees, culverts, and bridge abutments, help to reduce the hazard. Where light and sign standards are essential, these poles are designed to sheer or break off easily on contact. The best way to make sure that "force of impact" does not act upon your car is to drive at all times in a manner which will avoid collision with any and all objects!

The Force Of Gravity

Gravity — the force which attracts objects downwards towards the centre of the earth — will cause cars to lose speed going up hills, thereby decreasing their stopping distances; and to accelerate going down hills, thereby increasing their stopping distances.

A good driver will cut his speed when descending a hill; on steep grades, he should put his gear selector into Low, so that the engine of the car will act as a brake.

Hills are potential driving hazards for other reasons also. They limit visibility; the driver should not pass on or approaching a hill, no matter how slowly the vehicles in front are moving, unless there is a passing lane. At the crest of a hill, the driver must be alert for approaching cars not in their proper lane, or for obstacles in the road ahead, such as a car stopped while waiting to make a left turn. Remember that you must be able to stop your vehicle in the distance you can see ahead either day or night.

PASSING ON THE HIGHWAY

One of the manoeuvres of highway driving which requires the driver to remember all the physical laws of sight, friction, inertia, impact, and gravity, is the passing of slower-moving vehicles. Although passing certainly is a common manoeuvre, good judgement and skill are necessary. Here are several points to consider before passing another car:

1. How fast is the car that you are about to pass travelling?
2. What is the speed of your car?
3. How far will you have to travel in the left lane before you can pull back into your own lane?
4. What is the amount of clear passing distance ahead?
5. What is the speed of any car approaching you?
6. Is there enough room available to move back into your lane after you have passed?
7. Are there any vehicles about to overtake you?
8. Are there any other hazards which may exist, such as obstructions to visibility, poor road surface, etc.?
9. Does your car have enough power? (Cars with small engines require more distance in which to pass.)
10. Do the lane markings on the highway permit passing?

When all the above conditions have been considered and are favourable for passing, the manoeuvre is carried out in this way:

1. Leave a safe distance between you and the car being passed.
2. Look in the rear view mirror, and make a shoulder-check.
3. Signal your intention to pass (using the left-turn signal).
4. When clear, pull out into the left lane.
5. Tap your horn gently to warn the driver ahead of your intentions. At night, flick your headlights to high beam and back to low beam.
6. Accelerate to approximately 10 to 15 miles per hour faster than the car being passed.
7. At night, switch to high beam as you come alongside the vehicle you are overtaking.
8. Continue driving in the left lane until you can see the car you are passing in your rear view mirror. *Caution*: do not pull back into the right lane too soon.
9. Signal right and move back into your proper lane.
10. Check your speed to make sure you are within the speed limit.

When another car is passing you, there is a certain time in the passing manoeuvre called "the point of no return." This occurs about the time the other car is beside you. At this point it will take that car less time to accelerate and complete the passing manoeuvre than it would to brake and return to his place behind you. In the event of an emergency arising due to poor judgement on the part of the passing driver, you should brake your car in order to let him in ahead of you. This procedure may avoid a serious head-on collision.

Passing other vehicles must be avoided in any of the following situations:

1. Hills.
2. Curves.
3. Intersections.
4. Junctions.
5. Bridges.
6. Railway crossings.
7. Viaducts and tunnels.
8. Whenever the pavement markings forbid passing (see p. 45f.).
9. Pedestrian Crosswalks.

The skilful driver never passes unless there is ample visibility ahead, and all other conditions are favourable. By being patient and waiting for the proper time to pass, the chance of a head-on collision will be avoided.

LONG-DISTANCE DRIVING

We have discussed curves, hills, and passing manoeuvres – the seemingly more difficult of the driving techniques – but driving on a straight stretch of road requires just as much skill and attention. Many accidents are caused simply because drivers lose control of their vehicles which run off the road and collide with obstacles along the side of the road.

Before starting out on a long trip, the driver should be well rested and alert. High-speed driving requires *all of your attention*. Your eyes should be focussed well ahead on the road. By "side-scanning" the shoulders and sides of the road, impending dangers such as pedestrians, animals, cyclists, and other hazards can be seen and avoided.

Modern automobiles are fast, powerful – and very quiet. One does not get the feeling of true speed unless stopped quickly in the event of an emergency. Only then does this power become evident. Being wide awake and alert is your best assurance of being able to handle confidently any emergency situation that may arise.

"Velocitization" is a word which has been coined to describe a driver's sensation of non-motion after he has driven many miles at a high rate of speed. A driver must constantly guard against this sensation, glancing often at his speedometer and forcing himself to stay within the posted speed limits. Many drivers receive speeding tickets when entering built-up areas, towns, and cities, because they are victims of "velocitization" and simply do not realize that they are exceeding the posted speeds.

At the first sign of fatigue, you should stop well off the highway and get out of the car. Walking around or just relaxing by having coffee or a soft drink will refresh you and relieve tension. After this short relaxation period, you will go on your way again a much safer driver.

When driving along a highway, it is important to keep your vehicle centred in your proper lane. Do not become a "ribbon rider" (that is, a driver who persists in straddling the line down the centre of the road). Don't go too far the other way, however, so that your right wheels run onto the shoulder of the road at high speed.

Sometimes it becomes necessary to stop by the highway for emergency repairs. It is imperative that you move your car well off the travelled portion of the highway or onto the paved shoulder which is

provided on some highways. Many people have been killed or seriously injured when struck by other vehicles while changing a tire or making other repairs. If your car is equipped with four-way emergency flashers, turn them on to warn approaching traffic. Do not leave your directional signal flashing, as it may confuse a driver approaching from the rear — at night particularly, another driver may see a left-turn signal flashing and proceed to pass on the right side, only to find himself in an emergency situation. In some provinces it is illegal to use directional signals for this purpose.

If it is not possible for you to make repairs on the spot, raise your hood and tie a white cloth or handkerchief to your door handle. At night, turn on your inside courtesy light and wait for someone to stop and help you. It is dangerous practice to flag down approaching motorists.

HIGHWAY HAZARDS

There are many potentially dangerous circumstances or situations which can arise when driving on the open road. Some of these situations are discussed in the following paragraphs, along with suggestions for meeting them.

The Slowpoke Driver

This is the so-called Sunday driver who insists on driving much slower than the other traffic. He constitutes a real hazard. Cars line up behind him and become anxious to get by. Use care in passing the slowpoke. Wait your turn. Do not become impatient, and pass only when it is clear, and safe to do so.

Slow-Moving Vehicles

Farm machinery, and other slow-moving vehicles can also create a dangerous situation. These vehicles can be recognized by the triangular orange sign displayed on the rear of the vehicle. When you are approaching such a vehicle, slow down well in advance and pass only when it is safe to do so.

Construction Zones

When entering a construction area, slow down and be prepared to stop. Obey all posted construction signs and speeds. Watch out for flag-men who may stop you. Sometimes traffic may only move in one direction around the construction area and the traffic approaching from the other direction must wait until the way is clear.

Railway Crossings

Many people are killed each year on railway crossings. In some cases the motorists were trying to beat the train to the crossing. Other accidents have been caused by poor visibility. Some people, after stopping for one train, proceeded across only to be struck by another train coming from the opposite direction because they did not wait until the way was clear. When approaching railway crossings, slow down, check the tracks in both directions, and proceed cautiously when it is clear to do so. Many vehicles stop at all railway crossings, so if you are following such a vehicle, be alert and keep a safe following distance. Never gamble with a train at a crossing. You CANNOT win.

Pedestrians And Hitch-hikers

These pose a problem for highway drivers. If you see a pedestrian walking along the road with his back to you, sound your horn to warn him of your approach. Be particularly alert for children because they are unpredictable and may cross in front of you. Hitch-hikers are one type of pedestrian that a motorist should be wary of. You must use your own judgement in this situation: on the one hand, you yourself may have travelled by hitch-hiking, and it is pleasant to "return the favour"; on the other hand, well-meaning motorists sometimes pick up people who may be criminals, runaways, or mentally defective, who may cause the drivers trouble. Also remember that making a sudden stop to pick up a hitch-hiker can be hazardous to other traffic.

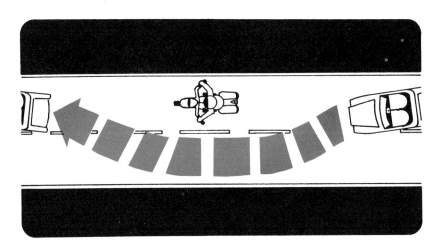

Motorcycles And Bicycles

When approaching motorcycles or bicycles on the highway, extreme caution must be exercised. When you are overtaking from behind, sound your horn gently to warn of your approach. Always pass to the left and allow plenty of room for the cyclist. When meeting an oncoming cyclist, slow down and pass well over to the right side of your lane. At night, be careful of a vehicle with only one light approaching you, since this could be a motorcycle or a car with one headlight. Slow down, stay well to the right, and exercise extreme caution.

Intersections And Highway Junctions

On highways you will encounter many intersections, crossroads, and farm lanes. All of these should be approached with caution. A vehicle may enter your traffic lane with very little warning, or a car may ignore a stop sign at a junction. Be prepared for any such emergency by observing all such crossings well in advance, and by driving with your eyes focussed as far ahead as possible.

Night Driving

The fatal-accident rate is about three times greater at night than it is in daylight. A driver's vision is poorer, and when visibility is reduced, the accident rate increases.

As a new driver, you must be aware of the potential hazards of night driving, and be ready to meet them with increased alertness. The headlights of your automobile provide good illumination, but you can still see only a comparatively short distance ahead. If you are driving at a high speed you may not be able to stop within the distance lit by your car's headlights. This is called "over-driving your headlights." This means that you would not see an obstacle in time to avoid hitting it. The only way to avoid over-driving your headlights is to reduce your speed at night. At 60 miles per hour, the average car and driver require a stopping distance of 270 feet under *ideal road conditions*.

Headlights on high beam allow a driver to read a sign at about 300 feet, again under ideal conditions. Thus there is little room for error, and certainly no room for greater speeds. Under poor conditions, car headlights will illuminate a much shorter distance ahead. What, therefore, is a safe speed to drive? (See the graph of stopping distances on page 89.)

Headlight glare from oncoming traffic also affects your vision. In some cases vision is affected for as long as 60 seconds after meeting bright headlights. (See Chapter 13, page 140.) To some extent you may be partially blinded for this period of time. If you are driving at 60 miles per hour, your car will travel almost a mile before your eyesight recovers fully. In addition to slowing down, you should avoid looking directly at bright headlights; lower your eyes to the right-hand edge of the roadway. The law requires a driver to dim his headlights within 500 feet of an approaching vehicle and within 200 feet of a vehicle he is following. A courteous driver will dim his lights before they become a hazard to the other driver.

DEFENSIVE DRIVING

What we are really discussing in all of the previous "Highway Hazards" is the need to develop the ability to "drive defensively." This means that you are not only in complete control of your own vehicle but you are keeping a careful eye on those drivers ahead, behind, and to the sides. In this way you will avoid being trapped in an accident-producing situation. *A defensive driver is always prepared for the possibility that other drivers may make errors.* Defensive drivers usually travel thousands of miles without once getting into a tight situation that may require an emergency manoeuvre.

PRE-PLANNING A TRIP

Before starting out on a long trip there are many things to consider. The condition of your car is very important. Here is a check list:
1. Make sure the tires are in good condition and properly inflated. Check the spare tire to be sure it is properly inflated also.
2. Check the lights, including headlights, brake lights, tail lights, directional signal lights and four-way flashers.
3. Check the wipers and windshield washers. Fill the washer reservoir if necessary.
4. Check the oil, and change if necessary.
5. Fill the gasoline tank.
6. Check the fan belt and power equipment belts. Tighten them if necessary.
7. Inspect the water level in the battery.
8. Check the coolant level in the radiator.
9. Make sure that all equipment is working properly (flashlight, jack, wheel-wrench, etc.).

   Good road maps may be obtained from your local service station. These show routes, mileages, and other details. A wise motorist will plot his trip on one of these maps in advance, so that he knows what highway numbers to follow, where junctions are, and where he will stop for food, fuel, and sleeping accommodation. Further information on highway conditions is available from various motor clubs or from your local government agency. *Caution:* never try to read or look at a road map while driving your car.

9

driving the freeways

In the previous chapter, we discussed some of the features and problems common to all highway driving. In this chapter, the topic is the particular form of highway known as the freeway, or "super-highway," as it is sometimes called.

Freeways are so-named because obstacles that delay traffic on regular streets and roads are non-existent: there are no intersections or crossroads, no left turns, no stop signs or traffic lights. Slow-moving vehicles, bicycles, and pedestrians are not allowed, and medians or other barriers separate vehicles travelling in opposite directions. But there are special problems to consider, and drivers must know the special techniques of freeway driving. Rates of speed are higher, and, if an error is made, the result is often death, serious injury, and heavy property damage.

"Driving on the Freeways" will be discussed under five main headings: Preparations; Getting on the Freeway; Freeway Signs and Lane Markings; Driving the Freeway; and Leaving the Freeway.

PREPARATIONS

The Driver

Driving on the freeway calls for constant attention. The speed limits are generally higher than on regular highways. Stopping distances are therefore much longer, and a slow reaction by the driver can cause a very serious accident. A driver should be in good mental and physical condition. The freeway itself is free from accident-causing situations, but if you are to profit from this advantage, you must be free from disabilities that would cause you to be a danger to yourself or to others.

Being prepared also means knowing how to get on the freeway, where to change to other freeways, and where to exit. When travelling in a strange area, have the necessary road maps and study them carefully before entering the freeway. If necessary, know the rest areas along the way. Knowing the names and/or numbers of exits is of first importance for a safe and pleasant journey.

The Car

Generally speaking, steady driving at a high rate of speed is actually less of a strain for a modern car than the stop-and-start driving of city traffic. There are certain problem areas, however, that are closely connected with highway driving:

1. Tires particularly are affected by prolonged high speeds. Before you begin a trip, be sure the tires are in excellent condition. Have them inflated at the proper pressure, and do not alter this pressure while they are hot.
2. Fan and power equipment belts should be checked for wear and for proper tension.
3. Coolant must be checked when the engine is cold. Fill the radiator according to the manufacturer's specifications.
4. Oil of a poor quality will not stand long hours of super-highway speed. Make sure that the crankcase is properly filled with high-grade oil.
5. The gas tank should be filled before starting, and, as in any other type of driving, refilled before the gauge goes below one-quarter.

GETTING ON THE FREEWAY

The Entrance Ramp

When nearing the freeway, be sure to enter the proper ramp for the direction you wish to take. On some freeways, the entrance and exit ramps are close together, and you may mistakenly move into an *exit* ramp and meet traffic coming out of the freeway, or else enter the freeway heading in the wrong direction.

Keep your speed within the legal limits, and always adjust speed to the conditions.

Merging With The Traffic On The Freeway

Some freeways have a clearly-designated acceleration lane that will allow the entering driver to accelerate up to the speed of vehicles on the freeway before attempting the merging manoeuvre. Learn to use the acceleration lane; accelerate and indicate your intention to merge well before you reach the lane's end. If you do not merge soon enough you may have to stop at the end of the lane and wait for a long gap in the oncoming traffic.

On freeways that do not have this special acceleration lane, a driver has to accelerate on the entrance ramp, find a suitable space, and merge without delay. In other cases, access to the freeway is controlled with yield signs, which leave the responsibility for proper merging to the entering driver. Sometimes there are merge signs on the freeway as well as on the entrance ramp.

Drivers who are already on the freeway can help by changing to the left lane if they see a slower vehicle merging from an entrance ramp. Always check for other traffic, first, however, to be sure that the left lane is free.

FREEWAY SIGNS AND LANE MARKINGS

Freeway signs are generally positioned above the roadway. Large letters and short messages are used, so that you do not need to slow down in order to read the information. The signs are usually repeated at the exit ramps. Lane markings also are above the roadway. These indicate which lane you should drive in, depending on whether you are turning or continuing straight ahead.

Which Lane To Drive In?

On a two-lane freeway (that is, a freeway with two lanes in each direction), the left-hand lane is for passing only. You should normally use the right-hand lane unless too much slower traffic would mean constant lane changes. However, when driving in the right-hand lane, be especially cautious and follow at safe distances when approaching exit or entrance ramps. The car in front may slow down without warning; some drivers will make an emergency stop on the freeway when they realize that they have reached or passed the exit that they should have used. If you pass your exit, do not back up, but continue to the next turn-off.

Near the entrance ramps, another danger is that the approaching drivers may not know how to merge with the traffic on the freeway; some drivers merge at reduced speed and force traffic to slow down abruptly.

On a three-lane freeway, through traffic should use the centre lane and leave the left lane for passing. The right-hand lane should be used by slow vehicles and vehicles entering or leaving the freeway. On some specially-designed freeways or metropolitan boulevards, you may see the following sign: "Right Lane Must Exit."

DRIVING THE FREEWAY

Signalling Your Intentions

Signalling your intentions well in advance is of the utmost importance on the freeway. You must allow adequate time to ensure that other drivers have seen your signals and know what manoeuvres you intend to make.

All lane changes must be indicated with turn signals. Before slowing down, you should touch the brake pedal to attract the attention of the following driver.

Following

The following distance between your car and the car in front should be *more* than one vehicle-length for every 10 miles per hour of speed. One easy method of estimating a safe following-distance is to watch the vehicle ahead of you pass some definite point in the highway, and then count normally to yourself "one thousand one, one thousand two." If you pass the spot before you finish saying those six words, you are following too close.

Particularly, avoid following too closely at exit or entrance ramps.

Passing

You must always observe all the rules for proper passing:
1. Be sure to keep proper following-distances.
2. If possible, pass in the left lane. Some provinces forbid passing on the right.
3. Make sure the driver in front of you does not intend to move to the left lane to pass.
4. Check that the driver behind does not want to pass your vehicle.
5. Signal your intention so that the car in front and the car behind will stay in line. At night, flick your headlights to high beam and back to low beam.
6. Increase speed and move to the passing lane. It is necessary to increase speed so as to spend the shortest possible time in the blind spot of the driver being overtaken.
7. Remain in the passing lane until you see both headlights of the overtaken vehicle in your inside rear view mirror.

8. Signal your intention to return to the travelling lane.
9. Return to the travelling lane and resume normal speed.

"Highway Hypnosis"

Freeways are often built in long, straight, flat stretches of road, away from cities, towns and villages, and in general, away from beautiful scenery.

In these circumstances, it is easy to let your mind wander. You tend to look inside yourself, to think about your problems, and forget about the task at hand. You may stare at the passing scene without really seeing it. If you do not react decisively, you may become drowsy and hypnotized by your thoughts.

Always make an effort to keep your eyes moving and your mind alert. Driving safely on the freeway calls for your undivided attention, and you must force yourself to give it.

Rest Areas

Rest areas present the same problems of merging traffic as do exit and entrance ramps, and the same rules of safety should be

observed. Rest areas are indicated well in advance. A driver should decide early if he is going to stop.

The rest areas can add greatly to the pleasure of your trip. Do not drive for more than one and one-half to two hours without stopping for rest and a warm beverage. Thinking about your passengers' comfort, you should stop regularly even if you do not feel that you need to yourself.

Before leaving the rest area, check the tires, have the gas tank filled if below the halfway mark, and check the oil.

Be fully alert when re-entering the freeway, and merge safely with other traffic.

Emergencies

Whenever it is necessary to stop along the freeway, remember the following rules:
1. Signal your intention.
2. Do not slow down in the travelling lane without giving sufficient notice to other drivers.
3. Move over to the shoulder as soon as you can safely do so.
4. Move your vehicle as far as possible from the travelled portion of the roadway.
5. Lift the hood of your car and attach a white cloth to the radio antenna or front door-handle.
6. Place warning signals and wait for help in your car (do not remain in your car if you are not safely away from the travelled lanes). Remember that you are not allowed to walk on the freeway. Police cars are constantly patrolling the freeways, and will call for the kind of help you need.
7. Returning to the freeway after an emergency stop calls for alertness. Observe the rules for proper merging with the traffic on the freeway.

LEAVING THE FREEWAY

Deceleration Lanes

Be sure you know the name and number of the exit to reach your destination, and change to the proper lane well before you reach that exit.

Do not decelerate on the through lane, but move into the deceleration lane as soon as possible, and slow down to the posted speed on the exit ramp. Do not depend on "feel," but look at your speedometer and reduce speed with care. Prolonged fast driving will reduce your "sense of speed," so that you cannot estimate speed accurately. You must check the speedometer to be sure you are travelling at a safe rate.

Freeways without deceleration lanes present a more difficult problem. Speed should be reduced on the ramps themselves, which are designed for this purpose. Unfortunately, inexperienced drivers tend to reduce speed on the through lanes, thereby causing a dangerous situation to develop; fatal collisions from the rear have been caused by this practice.

When driving in wintertime, the freeway ramps may be icy and speed may have to be reduced before turning into the exit.

Getting Back To City Driving

After leaving the freeway, the driver must get used to slow speeds, stop signs, traffic lights, and pedestrians again. A driver should remember that he does not have the alertness he had when he started his journey.

10

off the main route

MOUNTAIN DRIVING

Driving in the mountains can be an enjoyable adventure if you are willing to take the necessary precautions that are a vital part of safe, sane, defensive motoring. Steep hills, hairpin turns, a cliff on one side and a chasm on the other, may create a frightening and unnerving atmosphere if the driver is unprepared. Common-sense action will avert the majority of problems that may arise.

One particular problem of mountain driving is that fluid will boil at a lower temperature because of the decrease in atmospheric pressure as you increase your altitude above sea-level. The coolant in the radiator must be checked for quantity, and the thermostat for temperature rating. A low-temperature thermostat should be installed, and bugs, dirt, and leaves should be removed from the radiator vanes to improve the cooling.

Another problem is that of braking on long steep inclines. Steady pressure on the brake pedal has proven to be the best method under these conditions. "Fanning" the brakes is not recommended, since this tends to generate more heat in the brakes; on long slopes this will cause the brakes to lose their effectiveness, or "fade." Excessive use of the brakes can be alleviated by using second or first gear when slowing down. This manoeuvre utilizes the braking power of the engine and saves considerable brake wear. The lower gear should be selected before proceeding down the hill. Advance preparation eliminates many problems.

Before tackling the mountains, be sure your vehicle has sufficient power for the job. If your car is loaded down with equipment in the trunk, or if you are pulling a house trailer, you will need more power than you would normally require. Does your car have enough? Your auto dealer will advise you on this.

Mountain driving means a high-altitude atmosphere, which in turn means a decrease in the amount of air available for complete combustion. For steady mountain driving, the owner should investigate the advisibility of having larger jets installed in the carburetor. This will create a greater air flow to compensate for the lack of air at the increased heights.

Alternate routes must always be considered when driving in the mountains. Snow storms, snow drifts, snow and land slides, icy roads, fog, and other adverse conditions may force the driver to take the alternate route or else spend the time in visiting or sightseeing in the area rather than attempting to drive to his destination.

GRAVEL ROADS

Gravel roads create hazards not met on paved highways. The "washboard," very common on gravel roads, can make a car fishtail, and can even put the car in the ditch or into the path of an oncoming car. Braking distance is lengthened, as the gravel and stones will roll under the wheels, especially if the wheels are locked. Soft shoulders are common; there is a real danger that the car may be pulled into the soft sand and become stuck. Dust and flying stones from other vehicles also add to the driver's problems. Always increase the following distance on gravel roads to prevent collisions, stone bruises, pitted or cracked windshields, and broken headlights. These should be checked frequently when driving on gravel roads.

BUSH ROADS

Canada has an untold number of areas for the adventurer to investigate. With your car, you can reach a jumping-off point from which you can travel to the remotest areas by boat, canoe, trail-bike,

snowmobile, or snowshoe. Driving on bush roads and logging trails creates additional hazards to the sportsman and the adventurer, however. High crowns on the road may cover large boulders or stumps that can damage or ruin the underparts of the car. Keeping to one side of the road with the inside wheels on part of the crown will produce enough clearance to get by most obstacles. Also remember that sharp turns and short steep hills reduce visibility, and if another vehicle should suddenly appear, you will have very little time to take evasive action. Bush roads in lumbering areas are usually smoother, but on the other hand, you are more likely to be suddenly confronted with a huge truck coming right towards you.

Water-filled pot holes are another problem, as there is no way of knowing how deep the hole is unless you check it beforehand. If the hole is too deep, the surrounding brush may be used to fill the hole before proceeding.

Rain can make a bush road so slippery that the tires have little or no traction. A small hill can become the greatest obstacle on a bush road. Brush and evergreen limbs can aid traction in this instance. Bridges on bush roads are often in need of repair, were not made for automobile travel, and are usually quite old. The driver must cross all bridges with caution, and if in doubt, should not attempt a crossing.

Do not pass anyone stopped on remote roads without offering assistance. Nor would any true sportsman leave the travelled highways and roads without survival gear. Extra gas; a spare tire; a tow rope, preferably a pulley-type; an axe, food, chocolate, matches, flashlight and sleeping gear — all are necessities of life in the bush. If you are prepared for all eventualities, you will enjoy these excursions, and you will return safe and sound from every new adventure.

11

weather wipe-out

Driving in good weather is usually enjoyable. But when the weather turns bad, a driver faces many new and difficult situations which demand much greater skill.

In dealing with the problems presented by inclement weather, you must be aware of the conditions and prepared to compensate for any new dangers. Frequently drivers fail to recognize this change, and are taken by complete surprise when their vehicle fails to respond and react as usual, but goes into an unexpected skid instead. A good driver never allows a dangerous situation to develop if it can possibly be prevented. **Anticipate and react**, before the emergency arises.

VISIBILITY AND BAD WEATHER

In many types of bad weather, the driver's "clear sight distance" is seriously reduced. Always check the following items to make sure everything is prepared for any type of bad weather that might occur.

Glass

THE WINDSHIELD

Be sure the windshield is clean. The outside may be coated with dirt, grease, or slush and should be washed.

If snow or ice has collected on your vehicle, be sure to clean *all* the glass surface before starting your journey. Cleaning a "peep-hole" is not enough to give you proper sight in heavy traffic. Also remember that dust and smoke can leave a film on the inside of the windshield, which can reduce a driver's visibility.

THE HEADLIGHTS

Here again a film can collect, which will reduce the effectiveness of your headlights, and thus reduce your sight distance. Be sure to clean all driving lights regularly.

YOUR PRESCRIPTION LENSES

Frequently a driver who wears glasses will neglect to clean his "own glass," and will reduce his sight distance accordingly. Check this item carefully.

Window Cleaners

THE WINDSHIELD WIPERS

Be sure that your wipers are working and that the blades will clean without smearing. Drivers often neglect wiper blades, and the resulting film or "smear" will seriously reduce the sight distance.

THE WINDSHIELD WASHER

The windshield washer is a most helpful accessory for keeping your windshield clean. Be sure that you know how the washer is operated, and also check that there is enough fluid in the reservoir. If there is a danger of frost, be sure you have a type of solvent that will not freeze. It might be well to keep this type in the washer at all times.

THE HEATER-DEFROSTER UNIT

The heater-defroster will help remove condensation from the inside of the windshield at any time of the year, and should not be considered valuable only in cold weather. Also remember that your comfort, and possibly survival, could depend on your heater working properly. Be sure the heater is delivering the maximum amount of heat, and is working at top efficiency.

There are many situations which can affect your ability to see. If you cannot see clearly, then you must reduce your speed. Consider the following problem:

Suppose fog is so heavy that you can see only 50 feet ahead. At 20 miles per hour your stopping distance (including reaction time) is approximately 44 feet on dry pavement. What this means is that if you are travelling at more than 20 miles per hour, by the time you have seen an object on the road it will be too late to stop. Moreover, the fog causes a noticeable buildup of moisture on the pavement, so that the stopping distance is increased. Therefore, to be safe, you must reduce your speed to 15 miles per hour — regardless of what the posted maximum speed may be.

If your clear sight distance is reduced, you must reduce your speed to match. If you neglect this rule, you will find that you have created a crash-producing situation if any obstacle is in your path. You can only drive safely if you can see clearly.

With the following situations, decide how each would reduce visibility, and thus could be considered a potential hazard to your driving:
1. Darkness.
2. Dusk or twilight.
3. Fog.

4. Heavy rain.
5. Blinding snow.
6. Driving into bright sunlight.
7. Freezing rain.
8. Slush.
9. A tunnel.
10. A dust storm.

PAVEMENT PROBLEMS CAUSED BY WEATHER

When the weather turns bad your ability to manoeuvre a vehicle is diminished. Water on the road will reduce the friction between your tires and the road surface; you must compensate for this potential danger by reducing your speed in very heavy rain. Another point you should notice is that water mixed with oil and rubber creates an extremely slippery surface. Authorities warn that the first few minutes of a rain storm, especially after a prolonged dry spell in which an oil-and-rubber film has had a chance to accumulate, are extremely dangerous.

Observe how the coefficient of friction is reduced when you drive over mud at a road-construction site. Or perhaps you are driving on very wet leaves. In both these situations, the surface is very slippery, and you as the driver should be particularly cautious, and make sure your speed is appropriate for the conditions of the moment.

Ice and snow also reduce friction. Much experimentation has been carried on in these conditions, to determine how much longer it takes to stop the same car on various slippery surfaces than under ideal conditions.

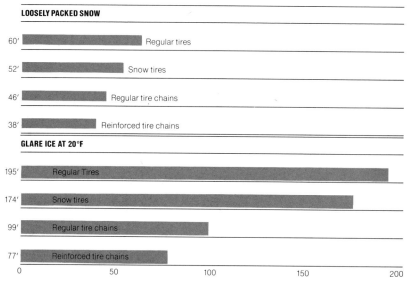

LOOSELY PACKED SNOW

60'	Regular tires
52'	Snow tires
46'	Regular tire chains
38'	Reinforced tire chains

GLARE ICE AT 20°F

195'	Regular Tires
174'	Snow tires
99'	Regular tire chains
77'	Reinforced tire chains

0   50   100   150   200

At 20 miles per hour the vehicle will stop in 21 feet (excluding reaction time) on dry pavement. On loosely packed snow, it will take 60 feet. However, on glare ice the distance to stop is increased to 195 feet — nine times as long as under normal conditions!

The stopping-distance chart shows only one of the hazards of winter driving. Frequently the width of the road is narrowed with snow drifts, and there is constant danger that fresh snow will cover ice on the road. These conditions can cause sudden and extreme danger unless you adjust your driving.

In the spring and fall, an early morning frost can create a deceptive slippery film on the road surface. In some areas, drivers are now warned about this danger, especially at bridges and overpasses. At these particular locations the temperature may drop more quickly, and the resulting frost can cause slippery surface conditions when there is little or no warning from observing other weather indicators.

In the spring you should note low areas on the road. Such areas will collect water, which may be covering a hidden patch of ice. Expert driving is demanded in this situation.

Brick or cobblestone pavement can be extremely slippery when there are small amounts of moisture on the surface. Since this type of pavement is frequently irregular, the amount of tire-surface in actual contact with the road at any given moment of time will be reduced. The resulting decrease of friction could cause a skid to result.

Gravel, sand, and washboard roads all need special care, since the irregular surfaces of these roads can easily lead to a loss of control. Wet steel rails on the road also have been known to cause unexpected grief when the driver failed to realize that the surface was extremely slippery.

A slightly different type of weather problem occurs when extreme changes in temperature cause the pavement to heave or crack, resulting in "frost boils" or the common pot hole. Pot holes and frost boils can cause you problems in a number of ways. Steering and tires can be damaged, and wheel-alignment thrown out-of-true. Hitting such an obstacle could also cause you to lose control of the car by the sudden lurch of the steering wheel. Be careful on such types of pavement. When you see posted warnings of rough or broken road conditions, heed them. Such warnings can save you expensive repairs, or possibly even your life.

In most of the above problems, your best procedure is to slow down. On slippery pavement it will take you longer to stop your car, so you need a greater following distance between your car and the vehicles ahead. Read your highway traffic legislation and see who is responsible for avoiding tail-end collisions. To say you slid into the vehicle ahead will not fix the damage or reduce your pain if you are injured. The only sensible thing to do is to watch constantly for dangerous weather conditions and drive appropriately. Always observe the following points:

1. Check the weather anticipated on your route.
2. Have your car prepared for bad weather or winter driving.
3. Carry grit, sand, or ashes to assist you if you become stuck.
4. Give yourself more time to reach your destination.

PREPARING YOUR VEHICLE FOR WINTER

Bad weather puts extra demands on your car, making it doubly important that all vital functions are performing properly. Check the following points:

1. Be sure the brakes are properly adjusted, and have good linings.
2. Check that the lights are working, and that the headlights are aimed properly.
3. Tired batteries die in cold weather. The resultant delay is irritating, and also is unnecessary. Always check the battery, and replace it when it is too old to do its job properly.
4. Be sure there is good tread on your tires — bald tires cannot grip slippery pavement. Better still, have snow tires installed to help overcome winter driving problems.
5. Make sure the windshield wipers are in good condition and properly adjusted. Add anti-freeze solution to the washers.
6. Check the muffler and tailpipe. A faulty exhaust-system that leaks carbon monoxide could kill you in any kind of weather.
7. Have the engine tuned up. Enjoy your winter motoring — don't be caught with a problem in the engine that could have been avoided with a simple tune-up.
8. Be sure there is anti-freeze in the radiator. Failure to attend to this small item will ruin your engine the first cold night of winter.

SPECIAL PROBLEMS PRESENTED BY BAD WEATHER

Brakes particularly are affected by bad weather. If you drive through water, be sure that you still have brakes that work. Check traffic, and when all is clear, try your brakes. If they do not react as you expect, hold them on for short periods of time so that the heat generated will dry them out. You should always know you have functioning brakes. If in doubt, check.

Another bad-weather problem is hydroplaning. This condition is caused when the water on the road makes a cushion for the tires to ride on. There is no coefficient of friction, and you have **no** control when such a phenomenon occurs. Studies show the problem can happen at any speed, but is most common in the mid-50 mile per hour range.

Never forget the pedestrian and the special problem he can create for the driver in bad weather. The major difficulty is still one of sight. It is sometimes impossible to see a person walking near or on the road in a bad rain storm, snow storm, or in fog. As a pedestrian yourself, be sure that you can be seen. Wearing something white at night can help the driver to see you, as is demonstrated by the photos on this page.

As a driver you must drive at a speed which will allow you to take any and all emergency measures that are necessary, no matter what the weather. If a pedestrian walks on the road because the shoulder or sidewalk is muddy, you still do not have the right to hit him. You will have a problem in seeing him, and the problem is never easy to solve. But as a driver **you** must take all the precautions necessary to care for the pedestrian on your route.

Another problem that can cause unexpected difficulties for the driver is that of high winds. Your car might suddenly lurch, and there will be a real emergency if you are not ready to steer the car and keep complete control. Both hands are needed on the steering wheel in this situation. A similar danger can be created by a large transport truck moving at high speeds. As the truck passes, there may be a sudden air blast that could present you with steering and control problems.

Entering a controlled skid in the practice area

SKIDS AND SKIDDING

Always do your best to avoid skids. In bad weather, when the danger of skidding is the greatest, you will need extra caution and care. If your car starts skidding, it is important to know what to do. Read the following steps, and note the diagram to show you the correct moves to make if your car starts to skid.

Steer

Skid

and away...

Turn steering wheel
in the direction the rear
of the car is skidding

First, keep yourself under control. Panic will not help. You really cannot control your car until you are acting correctly, and following the simple steps that will stop the skid.

Do *not* brake sharply, as this will lock your wheels, and extend the skid.

Steer in the direction that the rear end is skidding. Now, these words by themselves might mean very little, so consider the diagram which shows the back end of the car swinging to the right. You must turn your steering wheel to the right to gain control. Take this book, and hold it flat on your hand. Move the bottom of the book to the right. In your mind consider the consequences if your book were a car and you turned the steering wheel to the left. The motion already started would be accelerated. However, if you turn to the right you will continue to keep the front of the vehicle where it belongs, namely, in front.

One danger always present in a skidding situation is that the driver will *oversteer* the vehicle. Be sure to turn the wheel only enough to counteract the skidding motion. Once you have started the straightening process, be sure you steer so as to have your vehicle moving in a straight path again.

As a new driver, you might well ask how skids start. It is a good question, and the following list will give you an idea of the situations to be avoided so as not to get into a skid:

1. Driving too fast on curves.
2. Swerving suddenly.
3. Applying the brakes too suddenly or too hard.
4. Accelerating or decelerating suddenly.
5. Driving too fast on bumpy roads, or when crossing a road crown, railway tracks, or icy ruts.
6. Driving on the road edge.
7. Failing to anticipate ice patches under bridges, on overpasses, around shaded curves, or in other locations.
8. Not using snow tires or chains in extreme conditions.

All these points should show that you, the driver, must avoid situations where you can get into a skid. The idea of preparation is very important, and must be one of your first thoughts when the weather turns bad. Anticipating and avoiding the problem is an idea that you must put into practice each and every time you meet bad weather.

12

physical health and driving

For safety and the enjoyment of driving, good health is as important as the good condition of the car. When governments make car inspections compulsory, you may wonder why it is not mandatory to produce a certificate of good health before being issued a permit to drive. Some provinces call for such a certificate for school-bus drivers. Many companies and organizations have their employees' health checked regularly. But even with a certificate of good health in your wallet, there are times when you may not be physically fit to drive a motor vehicle. You should know about temporary illnesses, and turn the wheel over to a companion, or stop and wait until you are sure you are fit to drive.

TEMPORARY ILLNESSES

Fatigue

Fatigue may be the result of lack of sleep, of hard work, or of too-long periods of driving. Even professional drivers must take a definite number of hours of rest between driving periods — in fact, there are regulations which limit the number of hours they can drive at one stretch. A new driver, or a driver with little experience of highway driving, will become tired much sooner than a veteran of the road, and should take breaks more frequently. Fatigue dulls the mind, and increases perception and reaction time.

Avoid "stay-awake pills." The primary effect of such pills is to prevent a driver from recognizing the signs of fatigue. They give a feeling of over-confidence until eventually fatigue takes over and a driver is unable to cope with the driving task.

To prevent fatigue on a long trip, keep the following suggestions in mind:

1. Sit in an erect and relaxed position, with the seat at the proper distance from the controls.
2. Stop regularly. Eat and drink regularly. Take a nap if you feel drowsy.
3. Make sure that plenty of fresh air is circulating through the car.
4. Remember the rules of "how to look," and observe them at all times (see Chapter 13).
5. Plan your trip so that you will not have to drive in darkness if you have been driving all day.
6. It will help you to drive safely if you are considerate of your passengers. They have confidence in your judgement; keep them happy, and stop when tired.

Sickness

Head colds and allergy conditions may cause eyestrain and fatigue. High fever will dull mental and physical abilities. Like a toothache, these illnesses will take your mind off the driving task. When in such a poor condition, avoid driving.

Carbon Monoxide

Carbon monoxide is a deadly gas found in the exhaust of all gasoline engines. It is the result of incomplete combustion. A cold engine will produce more carbon monoxide than a warm engine; an engine in bad condition will also produce more of that deadly gas than an engine properly adjusted.

Carbon monoxide is odourless, colourless, and tasteless. At low concentrations it may cause headache, nausea, dizziness, and drowsiness. Even small quantities can cause brain damage. Concentrated in a confined area, it will cause drowsiness, unconsciousness, and death, unless artificial respiration is given promptly. Certain rules must be observed at all times to prevent its dangerous effects.

DEATH FROM CARBON MONOXIDE POISONING
CAN BE CAUSED BY

An exhaust pipe clogged with snow or mud

A defective muffler system

Running the motor in an enclosed space

1. Never start the engine unless the garage doors are opened.
2. Never warm up the engine inside the garage, but get the car outside immediately.
3. Always drive with at least one window partly opened.
4. Consult your owner's manual for the use of your heater in heavy traffic.
5. If you feel ill while driving, stop your car and get out into the fresh air.

CHRONIC ILLNESSES

Diabetics, persons suffering from heart diseases, epilepsy, or other chronic illnesses, and persons who have to take certain drugs may suffer fatigue, spells, or convulsions. These illnesses must be reported when applying for a driving permit. Such persons may in some cases be allowed to drive, but should avoid driving in heavy traffic, in bad weather, or on long trips.

Diabetic Statistics

According to a five and one-half year study done in Prince Edward Island, diabetic drivers get involved in significantly more traffic accidents than non-diabetics. They also incur a substantially greater number of major court convictions, and minor convictions as well.

Between January 1, 1963 and June 30, 1968, 346 diabetic drivers were matched against an equal number of non-diabetic drivers in the same age-group. The diabetics were involved in 91 accidents, while the drivers in the control group were in only 53. Twenty diabetics incurred major convictions, as against only eight in the control group. Forty-three diabetics had minor convictions, against 35 in the control group.

PHYSICAL DISABILITIES

Hearing

From the point-of-view of driving, there are two disabilities connected with the ears: deafness and Meuniere's Disease (loss of balance).

Tests can easily determine the extent of these deficiencies, and permits are issued with or without restrictions according to the results.

When a driver suffers from permanent deafness he is generally required to have his vehicle equipped with side mirrors. He must also compensate by checking his blind spots extra carefully, and being especially cautious at railroad crossings and in school zones.

Partial deafness can be temporary, because of infection or ear-ache. Too much noise in or around the car, closed windows, and lack of attention may also cause a driver to fail to hear the sirens of emergency vehicles.

A driver must remember that good hearing is very important for safe driving and that partial deafness is in some ways more dangerous than total deafness, because the driver who does not recognize his deficiency will not compensate; he may fail to hear danger signals, and a serious accident may result.

Bone, Joint, And Muscle Disorders

Problems such as a stiff neck, arthritis, or bursitis, may cause pain that can limit a driver's movements and cut down his efficiency, especially in an emergency.

Handicapped persons may be allowed to drive a vehicle with special equipment. Their licence may restrict them to driving their own vehicle only. Persons so permitted to drive have a very good safety record because they know their limitations and compensate by being attentive and by observing all safety practices.

Like so many other aspects of driving, the question of physical health is largely a matter of common sense. A person suffering from a chronic illness or impairment will very probably realize whether or not his ability to drive is affected; if it is, it is only sensible to make appropriate allowances, and take extra precautions as necessary. A temporary illness should be treated even more carefully, since the degree to which your driving ability is affected is unpredictable — your reflexes, concentration, and co-ordination may be impaired to a greater extent than you realize. Give yourself more time and space for manoeuvres, and don't drive more than is absolutely necessary until you are feeling better.

13

to see and be seen

In the previous chapter we discussed certain types of physical illness that could affect your ability to drive. In this chapter, we shall concentrate on the one physical quality which, for the driver, is the most important of all — good vision.

THE NEED FOR GOOD VISION WHEN DRIVING

Actions and reactions are ordered by the brain when a message is sent to it by one of the senses.

It is estimated that, when driving, more than 90 per cent of these messages are sent by the eyes.

If the eyes see the true picture of the situation around the vehicle, and the driver has the necessary knowledge and driving skill, his reaction will be correct for the circumstances. If the picture sent by the eyes to the brain is blurred or delayed because of a disability of the eye, the message will be faulty, and the reaction ordered by the brain may be the cause of an accident.

A driver must:
1. Know how he *should* see.
2. Know the abilities of his eyes.
3. Know the disabilities of his eyes, if any.
4. Have his eyes corrected or learn to compensate for eye disabilities that cannot be corrected.
5. Know the effect of speed and other factors on the seeing abilities of the eyes, and how to prevent errors that may result.
6. Remember that other highway users may suffer from eye disabilities, and therefore take steps to make sure that they can see his vehicle.

Licensing authorities have set minimum standards on seeing abilities of drivers. In some cases, the requirements vary according to the type of vehicle the driver is permitted to operate.

SEEING ABILITIES AND SKILLS OF THE EYES

Some disabilities of the eyes are due to malformation at birth, whereas others may develop through the years. In both cases, however, corrective lenses can make great improvements in vision. The most common eye problems are hyperopia (far-sightedness), myopia (nearsightedness), astigmatism (the inability to focus accurately), and presbyopia. The last-named of these problems, which primarily affects persons approaching the age of 40, makes it difficult to read or see fine details clearly. A person with this problem has to wear lenses to focus properly in close work or when reading.

VISUAL ACUITY

"Visual acuity" is the ability to see details clearly at any distance. For example, a person with 20/20 vision can read a letter 5/16 of an inch high at a distance of 20 feet, or a 5 inch letter (with regular print) at about 280 feet.

Normal visual acuity is 20/20. Some people have better than normal acuity; for instance, someone with 20/15 vision could see a 5 inch letter at 372 feet. Other persons have below-average visual acuity; a person with 20/60 vision, for instance, could read a standard 5 inch highway sign from only 93 feet.

Visual acuity should be tested for both eyes independently. It is important that both eyes should be approximately equal – otherwise the weak eye may not assist the other eye in the process of seeing. If the disparity is great enough, the brain may suppress the poorer image, and in effect the driver may become "one-eyed" without knowing it.

Professional drivers especially need good visual acuity. They spend long hours at the wheel, and often are driving heavy vehicles. It is important that they see well down the road so that they can match their speed to the conditions ahead, and so avoid hard braking followed by slow acceleration, which may cause dangerous disturbances in the flow of traffic.

PERIPHERAL VISION

Our field of vision has a central area (a cone of about three degrees) in which the eye is capable of resolving sharp details. This cone is surrounded by a larger area, in which the eye cannot make out detail, but can detect general form and motion. This is called *peripheral vision*.

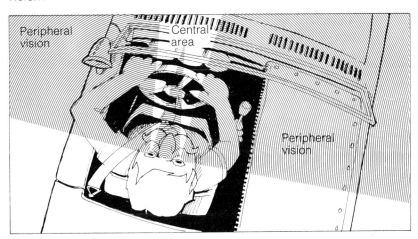

Peripheral vision is as important for safe driving as visual acuity. Although we look directly ahead when our vehicle is in motion, other users of the highway may move into our danger zone from the sides. Since our peripheral vision detects motion quite easily, our eyes are attracted towards the moving person or object, and we can take the necessary action to avoid a collision.

A driver with a normal field of vision can detect motion on his right and left for about 90 degrees, giving him a total field of vision of about 170 to 190 degrees. A restricted field of vision may be the cause of a very severe accident, if a driver does not see in time a car coming at an intersection on his right or left at a high rate of speed. Under the heading "How to Look" we will study the methods of compensating for such a disability.

All provinces have the same standard for peripheral vision, which is a minimum of 120 degrees in one eye.

DISTANCE JUDGEMENT

Distance judgement, as the name implies, is the ability to estimate the distance between the observer and an object, or between two objects.

The driver of a car needs to judge distances constantly when passing, following, turning left when a car is coming from the opposite direction, or when stopped and waiting to enter a main highway. A poor judgement of distances may have disastrous results.

To judge distances properly, a driver should have as close as possible to balanced vision in both eyes (ideally, 20/20 – 20/20), and also, training in judging distances. The instructor should show and explain how to use cues to judge distances.

Licensing authorities may or may not give a test on this skill of the eye. In fact, the test that is used is not a true "distance judgement test," but a test of *stereopsis*, which is a binocular visual perception of the three dimensions of space. Stereopsis will help in judging distances to close objects only, as compared with distances that have to be judged accurately in present-day driving.

COLOUR PERCEPTION

Deficient colour perception has not been considered a serious handicap to safe driving. However, there is a tendency to use colour more and more for signalling danger and conveying information (for example, red for "stop," yellow for "caution," green for "go"). "Colour codes" are also used to convey information on signs on some super-highways.

It is estimated that approximately 6 per cent of persons driving do not see the red and green of traffic lights. To help them, traffic lights are being standardized — red on top, green on the bottom. As an additional aid, some of the new traffic lights are made in the shape of highway signs. Thus, the red light is a square that looks like an octagonal stop sign from a distance; the amber light is diamond-shaped, to resemble a caution sign; and the green light is either round or uses arrows.

BINOCULAR CO-ORDINATION

Each eye is controlled by six muscles that move them in whatever direction we are looking. If the muscles of one eye do not work in good co-ordination with the muscles of the other, the eyes will not look at the same level or at the same point on a horizontal or vertical plane. This may result in blurred vision, double vision, or suppression of vision in one eye.

A serious defect in vertical or horizontal co-ordination should be treated, because the effort to attain muscle balance may cause confusion and fatigue.

NIGHT VISION

Night vision comprises three different functions:
1. The ability to see in low illumination.
2. Resistance to glare.
3. Recovery from glare.

Poor night vision, especially glare recovery, is characteristic more of older drivers than younger ones. All drivers should remember, however, that anyone may have to give up driving at night, no matter what his age, if his night vision is poor. We shall have more to say about night vision under the heading: "How To Look When Driving."

STANDARDS OF VISION AND YOUR LICENCE

How good your vision is may determine what type of licence you may obtain. The following chart shows the minimum standard of vision that applies across Canada.

CLASS OF LICENCE	VISUAL ACUITY	FIELD OF VISION	COLOUR RECOGNITION
OPERATOR OR CHAUFFEUR	20/40 Best eye	120° in one eye	Not mandatory
SCHOOL BUS	20/30 Best eye 20/50 Weaker eye	120° in each eye	Must recognize Red and Green

The Effect Of Speed On Vision

VISUAL ACUITY

One of the primary effects of speed is to decrease visual acuity for objects in the foreground, which are rendered unclear because of the motion and vibration of the car. Investigation has shown that this range of sub-standard foreground-vision increases by approximately 20 feet for each increase of 10 miles per hour in speed. Thus at 20 miles per hour we cannot see details clearly within 40 feet ahead of the car; at 60 miles per hour, not within 120 feet or more.

Let us imagine a driver with 20/20 visual acuity driving at 60 miles per hour. There is a highway sign ahead with three lines of writing on it. This driver does not know the area — his memory cannot be of any help — so he must read the sign. We have seen earlier that this driver can read 5 inch letters from 280 feet. We now know that when his car reaches a point 120 feet from the sign, he cannot clearly see the details. He has only 160 feet, or 1.8 seconds, to read the sign.

A driver with 20/60 vision cannot see that same sign before he reaches a point 93 feet from it — but his close-up vision is affected the same as the first driver's. Will this driver be able to read a three-line message?

This problem of reduced close-up vision explains why some drivers make emergency stops or slow down abruptly at road junctions, especially at super-highway exits. You must always be aware of this danger and be ready for any sudden action by other drivers. If you know the area you are driving in, a short glance at the sign will be sufficient — but remember that strangers who do not know their way will need longer periods of time.

Road departments, having studied this problem, use symbols as much as possible, or make the written message as brief as they can. Super-highways always have signs with large and easily-read letters.

FIELD OF VISION

Your field of vision is reduced by concentration and speed. When you concentrate on one single object, the field of vision is nil — which is generally what happens with new drivers, because they tend to stare at what they believe to be important.

Field of vision is also narrowed by speed. When stopped, a driver's field of vision may be as high as 190 degrees, but for the same person, the angle will be narrowed to 40 degrees at 60 miles per hour. That is why, whenever possible, highway signs are positioned above the roadway.

DISTANCE JUDGEMENT

Good distance judgement is dependent on good visual acuity. Since acuity is reduced by speed, distance judgement will also be adversely affected when you are driving fast.

Other Factors And Their Effect On Vision

AGE

Changes in visual performance are not restricted to advanced years, but depend upon many factors, general health being probably the most important. Increased difficulty in coping with glare, decreased sensitivity to light stimuli, and poor night vision are the usual signs of deteriorating eyesight. This does not mean that an older person with poorer vision cannot drive, however. With good experience, a driver can compensate for the problem and drive safely. If loss of vision becomes extreme, however, no one should wait for the authorities to take away his driving licence. A driver should voluntarily stop driving rather than risk his well-being and that of others.

ALCOHOL

Alcohol and certain drugs have an adverse effect on seeing, and also slow down reaction-times and affect muscular co-ordination. This particular topic is discussed more fully in Chapter 15.

GLARE

Daytime glare, either from direct or reflected light, will cause bleaching of the "visual purple" of the eyes and impair the ability of the eye to adapt to the dark.

The use of protective lenses against daytime glare will reduce the bleaching effect, and provide relief from discomfort. Sunglasses or tinted lenses should not be worn at night, however. They may prevent night-time glare, but they also reduce vision, depending on the amount of light they absorb. Tinted glass also reduces the distance you can see clearly ahead. At night, stopping distances become greater than seeing distances at high speed, even with the best possible night vision. It is only sensible, therefore, that a driver must not wear lenses that will shorten seeing distances even more.

FATIGUE

Physical fatigue hastens visual fatigue, which in turn slows down perception and reaction to stimuli, and may cause double or one-eyed vision, and lead to accident-producing situations.

ONE-EYED VISION

One-eyed vision may be permanent or the result of eye fatigue after driving excessive distances.

A driver with only one eye is not normally eligible for a chauffeur's licence, and cannot become a professional driver. He is also required to have a mirror on the side of the weak eye. He has to learn to compensate for this disability.

Drivers with good eyes may never notice that they see, at times, with only one eye – their dominant eye.

One-eyed vision produces many driving problems. Distance judgement does not have the assistance of stereopsis as it normally would. The field of vision is reduced on the side of the eye from which signals are not accepted by the brain, so that a pedestrian or object may not be seen or be seen too late to avoid a collision.

"HOW TO LOOK" WHEN DRIVING

No matter how well a new driver has succeeded on the vision test, he has to learn how to use his vision when driving. The proper techniques have to be learned and practised, beginning with his first lesson behind the wheel. They will become "seeing habits" that will make his driving safe and filled with satisfaction.

Where To Look

A new driver usually tends to look too closely in front of the car. Unless trained properly he may develop the dangerous habit of looking at the shoulder of the road, at or around the hood ornament, or worst of all, at the centre line, close to the car. It is well known that a driver steers the car in the direction he is looking.

This difficulty can be avoided by always having a "reference point" – a point as far as you can see down the road in the centre of

the lane where your car must pass. This reference point is always moving forward as the car is moving. Remember that your field of vision narrows with speed, and unless you turn your head right and left and try to keep a wide picture, you might not see any movement at the side that would have attracted your eye if your mind were not concentrated on a particular object. When you return your gaze to the direction straight ahead, your eye should again fix on the reference point. Normally, the eyes move automatically about every 1.7 seconds. When you stare, the natural movement of the eyes does not happen as it should, and your vision becomes glazed; "highway hypnosis" may result. Highway hypnosis happens mostly on roads that are flat, with no scenery to attract the driver's eyes. The driver who has not made a firm habit of moving his eyes every two seconds is very prone to this danger.

Every five seconds, at least, look in your rear view and side mirrors to keep track of what is happening behind the car. Look more often when traffic is heavy.

While driving in the city, you will have many reasons to look away from the reference point: the sidewalks, parked cars, intersections and intersection controls, the cars in front, the cars behind. Even then, if you are feeling under par, or are too busy with your thoughts, your mind may be totally absent from the driving task, so that you might not notice some dangerous situation, or see it too late.

Highway driving is no different in this respect. Obstacles may be far away, but the car is moving much faster, and danger zones are lengthened accordingly. You must keep control of your attention, and keep your eyes moving.

To recapitulate, the proper "looking habit" is: look at the reference point without staring; turn the eyes when they are attracted by movement, check the possible danger, and decide what action is to be taken; and look elsewhere to some other possible dangers. If the road or the side of the road does not present obstacles, move your eyes by habit, checking right and left, checking the rear view mirrors, the gauges, and dashboard, checking the scenery, etc., and then return to the reference point. Keep track of things in your field of vision by being careful not to let your eyes be trapped and retained on one specific object. Relax, deal with objects as they come, and get the full picture because you are getting the most of your field of vision. Like your attention, your vision should be fully under control.

Escape Route

Always think about an "escape route." Coming up to the crest of a hill, look to the right shoulder of the road to see if there is room to move out of your lane if a car comes the opposite way on the wrong side of the road. Do the same when rounding a curve. Be prepared to move to the left (or the right) lane to avoid a collision with a vehicle entering or leaving a super-highway.

The habit of having a reference point far down the road is very important; when distance visibility is reduced by hills or curves, you will automatically reduce your speed because your reference point is closer to you; it will not feel safe unless you know that you can stop your car within your sight distance.

DRIVING UNDER CONDITIONS OF POOR VISIBILITY

These conditions are many. Some of the worst situations include dusk and night driving; rain, fog, snowstorms, and drifting snow; sunshine and shadows; and driving towards the sun. These problems are discussed separately in the following sections.

Dusk

During this period of "half-light," the cone of central vision is not as efficient as in daylight, but your eyes are not yet prepared for night vision either. Professional drivers try not to drive during this period if they can help it. Whenever practical, they will stop and take a meal or a rest to help their eyes adapt to the dark. If you must drive, it is imperative that you reduce speed and be particularly alert.

Night Driving

At night the eye sees persons or objects by *contrast* — light-coloured clothing or objects stand out against a darker background;

or by *outlining* — dark clothing or objects are silhouetted against a lighter background. People, animals, and objects are more or less visible depending on the amount of light they reflect to the observer. It is well known that light-coloured clothing or objects reflect more light than dark-coloured objects, and so will be seen from a greater distance. But a driver cannot count on other people or animals to make themselves more visible. A driver never knows when his headlights will reveal — too late — a darkly-dressed pedestrian or a car parked without lights.

When driving at night, your reference point must be a little higher than the meeting point of the headlight and the pavement in the centre of your lane.

Peripheral vision suffers less than central vision at night. It is very important that you train yourself to use your peripheral vision extensively when driving in daylight so that it becomes a firmly-set habit that you simply carry on at night. Otherwise, you may use only your central vision in the narrow cone of light. This concentration of the eyes and attention reduces the efficiency of the peripheral vision. The eyes would not move as they should, and, because of that lack of movement, eye fatigue may set in. As we discussed before, double or one-eyed vision may result.

PREPARING YOUR EYES FOR NIGHT VISION

Your vision takes time to become efficient at night. It has been determined that it takes at least 30 minutes to get it to 80 per cent of its efficiency, and at least one hour to reach 100 per cent. You can lose a good percentage of this adaptation to the dark by just lighting a match or looking at streetlights or the headlights of another car. When you drive at night, therefore, always keep the following points in mind:

1. When meeting a car, look to the right of the road, higher than the point where the light and pavement meet, using your peripheral vision to detect possible motion.
2. Never drive at night when tired. Stop and rest.
3. Remember that distance judgement is much more difficult at night, because you may tend to over-estimate the distance between you and other cars, and under-estimate your speed. You must be especially alert when judging distances to red lights — this colour presents special difficulties, so allow plenty of space when following another car, and more space to stop than would seem necessary at a red traffic-light.
4. Traffic lights are difficult to locate in brightly-lighted areas. A driver should rely a great deal on his peripheral vision; by trying to keep the wide picture of the scene in front, his field of vision

will catch the movement of changing lights, which will help to locate them.

5. Some drivers like to follow another vehicle at night. This is a very good method of driving, especially on strange roads, because the car in front illuminates the way for a long distance, helps to locate dangers on the shoulders by outline, and in general, helps you to keep a steady pace. However, when you follow another car, you must keep more than what appears to be a safe distance; make sure you use your low beams only, and look on the shoulder of the road and not at the red rear-lights of the car ahead — this practice has been known to put a following driver to sleep.

6. Avoid smoking when driving. Smoke will reduce visual acuity, and leave a film of smog on the inside of the windshield if the car is not properly ventilated.

7. Have all the lights and the windshield (inside and out) cleaned. Visibility is reduced drastically by dirt or film on the glass.

8. Drive at a speed that will enable you to stop within the distance you can see clearly ahead. Some provinces have lower maximum speed limits at night than during the day.

9. Eat a chocolate bar, chew gum, talk with your passengers — keep your facial muscles in action and your eyes moving to help prevent eye fatigue and highway hypnosis.

Driving In Rain, Dust, Snow, And Fog

Three of these conditions present about the same problem: rain, snow, and fog all act as a *mirror*. In modern cars, in which the driver sits about in line with the light rays from the high beam of the headlights, the light strikes the drops of rain, droplets of fog, or the snowflakes, and is reflected back in the driver's eyes. If the low beams are used, the light is reflected down towards the road to give more light. In these conditions, therefore, the low beams only should be used. Fog lights are also helpful because of their extra-low position on the vehicle, so that more light rays are reflected on the roadway.

Heavy vehicles with high cabs give better visibility yet because of the position of the driver. It is a good habit to follow these vehicles at a proper distance on such nights.

Sunshine And Shadows

Driving in a wooded area or on city streets at the time of day when the sun makes patches of shadow with the bordering trees or houses can be very dangerous. Tinted lenses or dust on the windshield may prevent you from seeing persons, animals, or objects on or close to the road or street. Reduce speed, and remove your sunglasses if you are wearing them. The same advice is also applicable when entering a tunnel.

Driving Towards The Sun

When driving towards a setting sun, always use the sunvisors. A dusty windshield is particularly dangerous in this case.

When driving with the sun at your back, remember that the oncoming drivers have very poor visibility. It is advisable to turn your headlights on to warn drivers heading in the opposite direction not to move into your lane.

HOW TO MAKE SURE THAT OTHER HIGHWAY USERS SEE YOU

Remembering all that has been said about vision and visibility, you will understand that it is important to take measures "to be seen" by other users of the highway.

What measures will help other drivers to see you?

1. Motion will attract attention. Therefore, the signalling system of the car can be very useful for this purpose. Never use turn signals when flashing lights are required, however.
2. Whenever you use hand signals, remember to attract attention to your car by flashing your stop lights. The hand signal for a right turn is especially difficult to see for a driver following at night with low beam lights on.
3. It is a good practice to flash your stop lights when you want to stop or slow down. This signal is a must on super-highways, because following drivers are easily distracted from the task of driving, and otherwise may not notice that you are stopping.
4. The horn is a safety device and must be used if no other means will succeed in attracting attention. Used at the proper distance,

a short blast on the horn will convey your message and will be accepted with gratitude.

5. Headlights. Driving in daylight on the highway with low beam headlights on is a safety measure for the following reasons:

— With headlights on, your car will be seen from a much greater distance. This will help drivers coming towards you to judge distances more readily and accurately. Oncoming drivers won't take a chance to pass other vehicles if they see your lights.

— With present car-styling, it is not always easy to determine if a car in the distance is coming towards you or going away from you. This is important when you want to overtake and pass a vehicle.

— With low beams on, it is convenient to signal your intention to overtake and pass by changing beams, as in night-time driving. This changing of beams is visible in the mirror of the car in front.

— In cold weather, the heat from the lights will prevent the formation of ice on the headlights, and when darkness comes, your lights will give good illumination without delay. As mentioned above, only use your low beams in the fog, rain, or snow.

— Never use the parking lights when your car is in motion. Parking lights are meant to indicate that there is a *parked* car ahead; if you drive with these lights on, other drivers may make driving errors because you have misinformed them as to what you yourself are doing.

In this chapter we have covered one of the most important aspects of safe driving. As we discussed, there are several sides to good vision. It is vital that you be able to see clearly the driving conditions ahead, so that you can quickly and correctly react when necessary. It is equally essential that other drivers see you and know your intentions, so that they do not make incorrect driving decisions because they were unaware of your presence. Always remember that your vision will be affected by speed, light conditions, fatigue, or illness, perhaps without your realizing it. If you always keep these points in mind, you will find that driving is safer and more enjoyable as well — a worthwhile double bonus for such a reasonable precaution.

14

emergency survival

This chapter outlines possible situations which could happen at any time, when least expected, during your driving career. The defence suggestions are merely recommendations for the situation. Each problem varies as to detail, so the defence must vary according to the situation.

Correct Defence Means Survival

SITUATION 1

You are driving down the highway at 60 miles per hour approaching a curve when another car approaching from the other direction at 70 miles per hour crosses the solid centre line heading straight for you.

DEFENCE 1

Do *not* steer to the left across the solid line. Brake, and steer out of the way onto the shoulder to the right. Sound horn. Do your best to avoid fence posts, trees, etc.

SITUATION 2

You are driving a vehicle down a slight grade on a main highway at 50 miles per hour. Suddenly the rear right tire blows without warning, and the vehicle swerves to the left and heads for the centre white line. A car is coming the other way at 60 miles per hour.

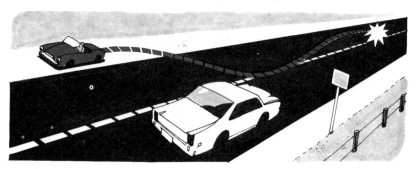

DEFENCE 2

Do not brake. Gain control of the steering and bring the car back on the correct side of the road. Let the car slow down without using the brake. Pump the brakes very gently at 10 or 15 miles per hour, and stop the car at the side of the road, off the pavement if possible.

SITUATION 3

You are driving down the highway in a 60 mile-per-hour zone when a car approaches from behind. This car tailgates but does not pass.

DEFENCE 3

Slow down so that the vehicle may pass. Reduce speed gradually. Get off the road if necessary.

SITUATION 4

Defensive drivers are always prepared for the unexpected. Imagine that you are driving down a main highway approaching an intersection with a secondary road which has a stop sign. Another car is approaching the intersection on your right at a high speed, and it appears as though the other driver will not be able to stop. What defensive action can you take?

DEFENCE 4

Slow down. Put your right foot over the foot brake. Be prepared to make an emergency stop if necessary.

SITUATION 5

You are travelling down a highway at night when your car develops engine trouble and starts to lose power. The car speed reduces to 20 miles per hour and the engine stalls.

DEFENCE 5

Pull completely off the road onto the shoulder, or onto a driveway or lot. Turn the emergency four-way flashers on. Lift up the hood. Tie a white handkerchief to the antenna or door handle. Use flares if you have them available.

SITUATION 6

You are driving down a highway when suddenly a car coming from the other direction pulls out to pass. It is apparent that he has not got sufficient room to complete the manoeuvre.

DEFENCE 6

Brake immediately. Pull over to the right. Leave the pavement and go onto the shoulder if necessary. It may even be necessary to go into the ditch if the other driver does not return to his own lane in time.

SITUATION 7

You are driving alone at night through a mountainous area where there are no motels. You become very tired about 50 miles from your destination. Gradually your eyes start to close for lack of sleep and you feel that you can no longer drive safely.

DEFENCE 7

Immediately stop the car in an area off the road. Shut off the engine. Get out of the car and take a short walk. Open the fresh air vents, wind the window part-way down, and lock the car. Sleep for an hour or two, providing that the temperature is not below freezing. When refreshed, drive on.

ADDITIONAL SITUATIONS

"What'll you do if...?" Things that shouldn't happen to a driver, but sometimes do.

1. The accelerator jams in heavy traffic?
2. The accelerator jams in light traffic?
3. Your car plunges into deep water?
4. The brakes fail?
5. A curve is entered at excessive speed?
6. A large animal suddenly appears on the highway?
7. The vehicle begins to skid to the left?
8. Fog, dust, or smoke suddenly obscures the highway?
9. You discover that your car is running out of gas?
10. The vehicle has gone through a deep puddle of water?
11. The temperature-indicator light comes on, or the needle on the gauge points to red?
12. You find you are becoming sleepy or getting a headache for no apparent reason?
13. The hood flies up as you are driving?
14. The engine catches fire?
15. Your door locks freeze?
16. Your vehicle breaks down on the expressway?
17. The red light for the alternator comes on or the ammeter shows a discharge?
18. You flood the engine?
19. You are stuck in a snow bank and have to wait for help?
20. You lose a wheel?

15

alcohol and other drugs

ALCOHOL: THE PROBLEM

In 1970, traffic accidents brought death to 5,197 Canadians, and injury to 177,930 more. Alcohol unquestionably was to blame for some of these crashes. Studies in various parts of North America show that a very high percentage of fatal crashes involved the misuse of alcohol. The Canada Safety Council suggests that alcohol shows up as a factor in at least 50 per cent of the traffic fatalities.

Most students realize that alcohol is used in a wide variety of ways in our nation. These include various industrial processes, medicine, perfumes, automobile radiator antifreeze, and also drinks of assorted flavours and strengths. This last variety of alcohol is called ethyl alcohol, and has the chemical symbol C_2H_5OH.

Many sincere people have put forward catchy slogans such as "Alcohol and Gasoline Don't Mix" or "If You Drive Don't Drink." Such messages have failed to point out the real danger involved in trying to drive when influenced by alcohol. Facts are always more impressive than slogans, so let us examine the facts about alcohol as they affect the automobile driver.

How Does Alcohol Affect The Human Body?

When you swallow an alcoholic beverage, the liquid first goes to the stomach. Here a small amount of it is absorbed into the blood. The rest passes into the small intestine, from which it is rapidly and almost completely absorbed, unchanged, into the bloodstream. Once in the blood, ethyl alcohol is circulated again and again throughout the whole body, passing through each and every cell and into every organ. This process quickly takes the alcohol to the brain. A person shows no effect from drinking alcohol until the alcohol reaches the brain. However we cannot simply state what the effect will be on any particular individual, since each of us is just that — an individual. The way alcohol acts upon you will depend on a great number of variables:

1. The type of beverage consumed.
2. The number of drinks consumed.
3. The rate of drinking.
4. The amount and kind of food in the stomach.
5. Your size.
6. Your condition: nervous, tired, excited, or tense.

When you consider the above list, it becomes clear that alcohol and its influence really is an individual matter. It is also a very complex matter, and a thinking person must understand the consequences if he tries to drive an automobile following the consumption of alcohol.

How do different types of beverage compare in alcohol content? In Canada, beer contains 5 per cent alcohol, wine 14-20 per cent, and whisky, 40 per cent. Expressed in another way, 1½ ounces of whisky is equivalent to 3 ounces of port or sherry, or a 12 ounce bottle of beer. Thus the type of alcohol consumed will be a variable in our consideration of the problem of "drinking and driving."

The *rate* of drinking must also be given serious consideration, since the more alcohol taken into the body in any given period, the higher the amount of alcohol will be in the bloodstream. Consider these facts. About 2 per cent of the alcohol is eliminated in the breath and in the urine, but the rest must be burned by the body in a similar fashion to fats, sugar, and other foods. Alcohol is burned only in the liver, and the rate of elimination takes place at a fixed rate. If a person drinks quickly, the liver cannot use up the alcohol, and thus the body builds up a concentration of alcohol in the bloodstream.

This fact of the fixed rate of disposal by the liver is important because the person who drinks and drives should consider the time necessary to use up the alcohol, and wait until a sufficiently low blood-alcohol level is reached so as not to harm or affect his driving.

From the available information it appears that the concentration of alcohol is related to the size of the person. A person who weighs 100 pounds will have a higher concentration of alcohol with the same intake than a person who weighs 180 pounds. Many people either do not know this fact, or else they disregard it.

Still another variable is the material present in the stomach when drinking begins. As noted previously, the alcohol quickly reaches the blood stream through the walls of the stomach or in the small intestine. If the person has food in his stomach, especially food rich in protein and fat, the rate of absorption of alcohol into the blood is reduced. When the stomach is empty there is little to prevent the alcohol from passing into the intestine. This accounts for the marked effect that can be obtained from a few drinks on an empty stomach at a cocktail party.

The last of the variables in our list is the tenseness or nervousness of the drinker. This point is frequently overlooked when considering the topic of alcohol and driving. When a person is nervous or tense, a passageway from the stomach called the *pyloris* may be restricted or even closed. When this happens, the alcohol remains for a longer time in the stomach, and thus will enter the blood stream at a slower rate.

However a note of caution should be made here. When the pyloric muscle relaxes, the alcohol accumulated may "hit" the system with all its accumulated (if drinking has continued) potency. If this happens, the person may very suddenly become intoxicated.

Research has shown that the human organism can handle the alcohol contained in approximately one ounce of seventy proof whisky per hour. This figure might be considered as a minimum-to-average rate of removal, but it too can be upset by such human factors as chills, poor circulation, fever, or unconsciousness.

Accepting the variables which are present in each human, let us turn our attention to how alcohol, once in the bloodstream, affects the brain and the physical functions of the body.

The first and most important action of alcohol on the brain appears to be on the "mid-brain," which acts as a sort of control

"Could you suggest something to ensure an evening of frolic and revelry . . . within a lega breathalyzer reading?"

panel through which all the functions of the different parts of the brain are directed. The mid-brain is the area through which conscious thought-processes are interconnected with emotional reactions, voluntary movements, and the functions of certain automatic centres regulating the action of the heart, breathing, the blood vessels, the movements of the stomach and intestinal tract, and so on. For this reason the first effect of alcohol is to interfere with the normal regulation by which all of these processes are connected to each other. The early flushing of the skin, excessive laughing or crying, the rapid jumping about of thoughts from one subject to another, are all signs of this loss of emotional control. Only at higher concentrations of alcohol is there actually an impairment of the ability to think or to carry out specific muscular activity. For this reason, a person who has drunk more than he should may still be able to walk a straight line when ordered to do so by a police officer, since a situation such as this would be serious enough that the person would be able to keep his attention from wandering. In a situation such as normal driving, however, the same person might be unable to keep his attention long enough on the same task to be a safe driver. This is one of the real problems of driving after drinking.

Because of variations among individuals, it is impossible to blanket all possibilities when discussing the effect of alcohol. However, it is safe to say that alcohol is an anaesthetic rather than a stimulant and will dull the working of the brain and nervous system. Also it produces a measurable impairment of a person's awareness, discrimination, and speed of reaction; this impairment is greater when a person is performing tasks which are more complex and which are more recently learned. The driving of a motor vehicle is complex, and for young drivers is "recently learned." Thus even relatively small amounts of alcohol may interfere with the ability to drive correctly and safely.

Add to this the adverse effect caused by loss of judgement and self-control, plus the change of a driver's attitude, and it should be easy to see that driving after drinking can lead to a great deal of trouble on the roads of our nation.

How much alcohol will affect a driver? Again we must remember the variables, and the difficulty that exists in generalizing about the average person. As an approximate guide, however, the following chart will help to show the effect of the rapid consumption of beer.

The figures given are roughly accurate for a person weighing 150 pounds consuming the stated quantities of alcohol over a one-hour period. The effect of other alcoholic drinks can be figured from this.

Amount of Beer	Blood-Alcohol Reading	Signs to Notice
1 bottle	.025	Little noticeable effect
2 bottles	.050	Flushing of the skin becomes noticeable. Inhibitions begin to disappear. The heart speeds up. Unusual gaiety is exhibited.
3 bottles	.065	Judgement is slower. Giddiness becomes apparent. Co-ordination is reduced
4 bottles	.095	Vision is a bit blurred. Speech becomes slightly fuzzy. Reaction time is slowed. *It is illegal to drive at this point.*
8 bottles	.180	Staggering and loss of balance becomes apparent. The person tends to see double.
12 bottles	.275	Co-ordination is severely impaired.
20 bottles	.450	The skin becomes clammy. The pupils are dilated. Unconsciousness sets in.

The Effect Of Alcohol On Driving

It now remains to see what the significance of this effect would be on a person's ability to drive. Instructions issued to one of the police departments contained the following list of characteristics exhibited by drivers who consumed unsafe quantities of alcohol:
- driving unreasonably fast; driving unreasonably slowly; in spurts;
- frequent lane-changing, then fast, then slowly;
- improper passing with insufficient clearance; taking too long or swerving too much in passing — this suggests over-control;

— overshooting or disregarding traffic control signals; approaching signals unreasonably fast or slowly; and stopping or attempting to stop with uneven motion;

— driving at night without lights; delay in turning lights on when starting from a parked position; failure to dim lights to oncoming traffic;

— driving in lower gears without apparent reason, or repeatedly clashing gears;

— jerky starting or stopping;

— driving too close to shoulders or curbs, appearing to hug the edge of the road, or continually straddling the centre line;

— driving with windows down in cold weather; and driving or riding with head partly or completely out of the window.

DRINKING AND HIGHWAY SAFETY

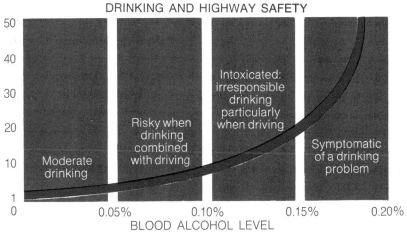

Number of 1 oz. drinks of 86 proof whiskey
for 160 lb. man within 2 hours of eating

Much has been written recently about the use of the "breathalyzer" in showing the true blood-alcohol level of a driver. Such a machine will assist law enforcement officers to identify any person who is a hazard on our roads.

The breath test must be done on an instrument approved by the Attorney-General of Canada, and a qualified technician must administer the test. The instrument itself is small and simple to operate. The

subject blows into a thin tube which leads into a cylinder contained in the machine. The last part of his exhaled breath – a "deep lung sample" – is trapped for accurate analysis of alcohol content, which is directly proportionate to the alcohol in the blood stream of the subject. This deep lung sample is then bubbled into a pre-tested ampoule which contains a chemical solution sensitive to the presence of alcohol. This solution is strong yellow in colour. Alcohol causes it to become paler. The breathalyzer then measures the decrease in the yellow colour by passing light through the solution. The intensity of the light passing through will be greater than that passing through another untouched control ampoule contained in the breathalyzer. The difference in readings is registered on the machine, giving the amount of alcohol present in each 100 millilitres of the subject's blood.

The subject is given the benefit of the doubt in breathalyzer tests.

Although his breath may register .088 alcohol consumption, the reading is rounded out to the nearest low unit of ten, which in this case would be .08. Two samples of the subject's breath are tested to make sure of complete accuracy. Usually the tests are spaced about 15 minutes apart.

The breathalyzer is also helpful to police to detect people who may appear to be intoxicated but who are really suffering from epilepsy, concussion, heart attack, diabetes, or overdoses of insulin or other drugs. If the subject registers little or no alcohol in his system, the police can then take immediate steps to get medical attention for him.

Results from the breathalyzer are accepted in courts in every province in Canada. Under the new amendments to the Criminal Code of Canada which became law on December 1, 1969, Section 236 reads as follows:

> Everyone who drives a motor vehicle or has care or control of a motor vehicle, whether it is in motion or not, having consumed alcohol in such a quantity that the proportion thereof in his blood exceeds 80 milligrams of alcohol in 100 millilitres of blood, is guilty of an offence punishable on summary conviction and is liable to a fine of not less than fifty dollars and not more than one thousand dollars or to imprisonment for not more than six months or both.

In layman's language this means that if you show a reading on the breathalizer of .08 or higher, you are "guilty of an offence." Considerable thought was given to the level of alcohol that would be officially defined as unacceptable, but research showed that a person with a reading of .08 was not able to function effectively as a driver of an automobile. It is worth noting that in some European countries the point of conviction is .05 rather than .08.

The amendments of the Criminal Code not only established the .08 law, but changed the Code in Sections 234 and 235 as follows:

> Section 234. Every one who, while his ability to drive a motor vehicle is impaired by alcohol or a drug, drives a motor vehicle or has the care or control of a motor vehicle, whether it is in motion or not, is guilty of an indictable offence or an offence punishable on summary conviction and is liable:

(a) for a first offence, to a fine of not more than five hundred dollars and not less than fifty dollars or to imprisonment for three months or to both;

(b) for a second offence, to imprisonment for not more than three months and not less than fourteen days and

(c) for each subsequent offence, to imprisonment for not more than one year and not less than three months.

Section 235. (1) Where a peace officer on reasonable and probable grounds believes that a person is committing, or at any time within the preceding two hours has committed, an offence under section 234, he may by demand made to that person forthwith or as soon as practicable, require him to provide then or as soon thereafter as is practicable a sample of his breath suitable to enable an analysis to be made in order to determine the proportion, if any, of alcohol in his blood, and to accompany the peace officer for the purpose of enabling such a sample to be taken.

(2) Every one who, without reasonable excuse, fails or refuses to comply with a demand made to him by a peace officer under subsection (1) is guilty of an offence punishable on summary conviction and is liable to a fine of not less than fifty dollars and not more than one thousand dollars or to imprisonment for not more than six months, or both.

Thus the government of Canada has begun a campaign to try and stop the "drinking driver" from remaining on our highways.

This new approach to the alcohol problem is causing much discussion in Canada to-day. Some argue that it is too tough, others that the law is still not rigid enough. It seems from the evidence now available that responsible young drivers who seriously consider the entire topic of drinking and driving and the consequences, will discuss all relative facts and will decide and act accordingly. When this happens, we can hope to see considerable improvement in our accident statistics.

For an interesting and valid comparison, Canadians would do well to examine closely the drinking-driving legislation in Norway for further discussion on this topic. Professor Nils Christie of Oslo wrote that "If a driver's blood-test measures above the legal minimum (.05

per cent in Norway) he will typically draw 21 days in prison and have his licence suspended for one year on the first offence (more on succeeding offences). . . ." He goes on to note that more than 2,000 persons were imprisoned in Norway in 1963 for drunk driving – in fact, more people are imprisoned in Norway for drunk driving than for all other crimes put together. A sizeable part of the Norwegian people at some time in their lives go through society's most severe ceremony of degradation – imprisonment with criminals.

We do not have space here to explore fully the problem of the alcoholic driver on our roads. But certainly this individual cannot be forgotten in any study of this topic. He is a hazard, and the thoughtful student should examine the definition of "alcoholic", and consider the danger presented by this person when he or she puts a car into motion on our roads. More study is needed, and licencing and enforcement officials must continue their vigilance to curb the driving activities of the alcoholic.

DRUGS AND DRIVING

It is a criminal offence in Canada to drive a motor vehicle when your ability to drive safely is impaired by a drug or drugs.

The complicated act of driving demands the complete functioning of all mental and physical parts of the human body. Both mental and physical functions, however, can be impaired by certain drugs. Whether the impairment will be large or small cannot always be predicted, as the action of drugs on the human body is affected by many factors. One of the most unpredictable factors is the individual's reaction to mixtures or combinations of drugs, or to drugs and alcohol.

To many drivers the term *drug* is used in relation to those substances which lead to addiction. However there are many preparations, sold with or without a physician's prescription, which can seriously impair your mental and physical functions. Such impairment might be called the "sneak drug attack." You do not set out intentionally to produce a reaction, yet your ability to drive is seriously reduced.

It is not possible in this book to list all drugs which can impair your ability. It is important for you to know the dangers that can exist, and also remember that you should ask your physician or pharmacist if it is safe for you to drive a vehicle while taking certain drugs. As a guide, the classes of drugs listed in this chapter may impair your mental and physical functions.

Narcotics

As narcotics can relieve pain and produce sleep, they sometimes are present in prescription drugs dispensed for coughs, colds, and pain. However, some cough, cold, and pain-relieving preparations that contain quantities of the narcotic *codeine* are sold without a prescription. Narcotics may be a potential hazard for drivers, as they produce drowsiness, defects in vision, and an inability to think correctly, concentrate fully, and react quickly.

Antihistamines

Antihistamines are used for the treatment of various allergic conditions such as hay fever, skin rashes, and drug allergies. Sleeping pills, cold preparations, motion-sickness pills, muscle relaxants, and other drugs may contain an antihistamine as one of their ingredients.

The most common side-effect of antihistamines is drowsiness. Drowsiness can disturb the proper functioning of the mind to such an extent that accidents can result. Other effects of antihistamines, such as blurred vision, lack of co-ordination, and excessive fatigue, add to the hazards of driving. If you are taking an antihistamine, be sure you know how it may affect your ability to drive.

Tranquillizers And Sedatives

These drugs have a calming effect. They are used for muscle relaxation, and in the treatment of tension, nervousness, epilepsy, sleeplessness, high blood pressure, and other ailments.

Again, as these drugs may produce drowsiness, blurred vision, dizziness and lack of muscle co-ordination, a driver must realize the problem and not drive.

Anti-Infectives

Possible side-effects of antibiotics and sulfas are dizziness, drowsiness, and impaired hearing, as well as nausea and vomiting. Your ability to drive may be reduced if you are taking a drug in this class. Be sure to check with your physician about any possible effects on your driving.

Hallucinogens

Drugs which induce dreams or achieve total escape from reality need to be avoided. Legally these drugs are available only to qualified persons. But many of them are sold on the illegal drug market, and there is certainly no medical warning given under these circumstances.

The very purpose of these drugs is to create hallucinations and disturbances of vision. To drive under their influence could be catastrophic.

Stimulants

Drugs in this group, including certain amphetamines, act directly as a stimulant on the central nervous system. They are prescribed to reduce appetite, to treat cases of depression, to correct behaviour problems, to counteract the effects of sedatives and drug overdosages, and to treat some types of epilepsy and muscle weakness.

Drugs in this group are referred to by many names, perhaps the most descriptive of which is "speed." Such drugs may temporarily increase your efficiency and alertness by masking the body's normal protective symptoms of drowsiness. The aftermath, however, is often collapse, which may be preceded by headache, dizziness, agitation, irritability, or decreased powers of concentration.

Since the body develops a tolerance to these drugs, the drug abuser tends to increase his dosage. The normal effects are exaggerated, with excitability, restlessness, nervousness, and aggressive behaviour being possible. This group of drugs is dangerous under any conditions and can certainly affect a person's driving habits.

The drug problem as it relates to driving is only now being thoroughly researched. In a Canadian publication entitled "Facts About Amphetamines," the author makes the following observations:

> Those who drive risk accidents caused by this aggressiveness, or by dizziness, delusions, hallucinations, or exhaustion. There is evidence that amphetamine abusers have even higher traffic accident rates than abusers of alcohol, barbiturates or tranquillizers.

Why Some People Take Drugs

To Combat Fatigue	To Erase Worries and Tensions	To Improve Mood
– caffeine	– alcohol	– alcohol
– cocaine	– tobacco	– narcotics
– amphetamines	– chlordiazepoxide	– amphetamine
	– barbiturates	– meprobamate
	– narcotics	
	– meprobamate	
	– bromides	

To Induce Sleep	To Achieve Total Escape	To Induce Dreams
– alcohol	– alcohol	– morphine
– chloral hydrate	– barbiturates	– cocaine
– paraldehyde	– paraldehyde	– mescaline
– barbiturates	– bromides	– lysergic acid diethylamide (LSD)
– narcotics	– narcotics	– marijuana

From the evidence, traffic investigators now feel that drug users are an extreme hazard on our highways. The person who takes drugs under medical supervision can have unexpected trouble, and should be aware of the dangers. The drug abuser takes drugs of many sorts to feel "different." Illusions, hallucinations, drowsiness, irritability, intoxication, impaired depth-perception, and other effects obviously make the driver unable to cope with the normal traffic complications of to-day. These problems are further aggravated if a combination of drugs or drugs and alcohol are used simultaneously.

The classes of drugs that have been mentioned and that have the power to produce undesirable side-effects are not by any means the only ones which may impair your driving ability. Many other medicines can affect a person's capabilities. Even some stomach preparations, eye drops, headache tablets, diabetes drugs, and others may affect your ability to drive.

Driving is sufficiently complicated without impairing your ability by misuse of drugs.

16

the law and its applications

A driver's responsibility is to know the law in any jurisdiction in which he drives. Ignorance of the law is not an excuse or a defence.

Traffic laws vary from province to province and even from municipality to municipality within a province. These variations in traffic laws come about because of local traffic problems and sometimes because of local preferences. The driver must remember he is bound by the laws of the area in which he is driving. He must be aware of and obey all laws at all times to drive safely.

WHY HAVE LAWS?

Fifty years ago, motor vehicles in Canada were numbered in the hundreds, and very few laws were necessary. By the decade of the Seventies, however, we have millions of motor vehicles, and in order to have traffic flow safely and smoothly, organization and control is necessary. Voluntary traffic rules would be the ideal, but unfortunately, human shortcomings make this impossible.

WHO MAKES LAWS GOVERNING DRIVERS?

Laws are enacted by every level of government, federal, provincial, and municipal.

The Federal Parliament

Under authority of the British North America Act, the Federal Parliament enacts the Criminal Code. There are several offences under the Criminal Code which may be committed while driving:

1. Criminal Negligence (Sections 202-203, 204-219).
2. Failing to stop at the scene of an accident (Section 233).
3. Dangerous Driving (Section 233).
4. Driving while under the influence of alcohol (Sections 234, 235, and 236).
5. Section 238 provides for the withdrawal of driving privileges for certain offences, and makes this loss of driving privileges apply to all of Canada, no matter what province or territory the offence was committed in.

The Provincial Parliament

The provincial legislatures produce the main body of law governing the movement and control of motor vehicles. This body of law is in the form of several statutes and their regulations. The most important of these are examined in the following paragraphs.

THE HIGHWAY TRAFFIC ACT

The Highway Traffic Act outlines the rules of the road and regulates actual movement of vehicles. This statute may have slight variances from province to province, but in general follows a Uniform Vehicle Code which tends to give uniformity to laws in all provinces as well as in other countries. An example of this is driving on the right-hand side of the road in North America. An exception is the making of a right turn on a red light, which is legal in some provinces but not in others.

REGULATIONS UNDER THE HIGHWAY TRAFFIC ACTS

Another part of the body of the provincial law is made up of regulations made under authority of the Highway Traffic Act. "Regulations" are those parts of the law which do not have to be approved by a meeting of the provincial Parliament. The regulations need only to be approved by the Lieutenant Governor in Council of the province and be publicized in the Provincial Gazette to become law. Regulations usually cover topics which may change frequently, or do not warrant a permanent part in the statutes, or are of such a technical nature that experts outside Parliament must decide upon their existence and modification. An example would be the regulations for tire specifications, which must be changed as new technical developments occur.

THE NEGLIGENCE ACT

This Act outlines the law on the occurrence of an accident when damage must be assessed and recovered. It allows for the sharing of costs between one or more persons found at fault or negligent, and it protects the innocent car owner from liability to passengers.

THE SUMMARY CONVICTIONS ACT

This Act provides for any occurrence in which drivers must be charged with some offence. The method of notification or "service of summonses" is dealt with, as well as a section where, upon notification, the charged person may plead guilty and pay a fine without appearing in court.

The Municipal Courts

Local governments are given power under the Highway Traffic Act to make laws for their own locality. This body of law regulates such matters as parking and traffic-control on the local scene.

Municipal by-laws usually are very standardized, and except for speed limits and traffic controls (stop lights, signs, etc.) which are posted, the law seldom varies. But there are always exceptions, and the driver's responsibility is to know them.

How do you, as a beginning driver, learn what the law is?

First, study the provincial Driver's Handbook, and for additional information, check the provincial Highway Traffic Act, their regulations, and local by-laws. The local police department will be able to supply details on the last-mentioned.

WHO ENFORCES DRIVING LAWS?

The Royal Canadian Mounted Police

The R.C.M.P. police all federal crown lands, such as federal parks, Crown Corporation property, and crown territories. Some provinces by contract with the federal government have the R.C.M.P. enforce the law in their territory.

Provincial Police Forces

The provinces of Ontario and Quebec have their own provincial police forces to enforce laws within the provinces except on federal crown holdings and within municipalities which have their own police force.

Municipal Police

Many larger municipalities have their own police forces. The municipal police officer enforces the law within the boundaries of his own municipality. A police officer may at any time take action against offenders, regardless of whether or not he is in uniform or on duty.

Parking-Meter Attendants

In order to relieve the police officer of routine duties so that he can concentrate on more important matters, some municipalities hire parking-meter attendants. These men and women have limited authority; their duties are to check parking and issue tickets for violations in this matter only.

The Ordinary Citizen

Any citizen may be asked by the law enforcement officer for assistance, and he or she is bound by law to give that assistance to the best of his or her ability. It must be pointed out that anyone assisting a police officer on request has the same protection from liability, and insurance in case of injury, as does the policeman himself.

A citizen witnessing an offence may, if there is sufficient evidence, go to the local police department and lay an *information* against the perpetrator of that offence. The person laying this information would then give evidence as a policeman would in court.

METHODS OF ENFORCING TRAFFIC LAWS

Traffic laws are necessary, but they will only be effective in making our roads and highways safe if they are obeyed. Voluntary obedience to laws would be ideal, but unfortunately impractical, since there are always people who think they are above the law or that the law is made for others. Therefore, enforcement is necessary; some of the methods are discussed below.

Police Patrols

Patrolling is done by police officers, usually in well-marked cars, who enforce the law by issuing tickets to offenders and by inhibiting potential offenders on the roads.

Air Patrols

Where traffic is heavy and control is difficult with only highway patrols, these patrols are supplemented by aircraft which can get an overall view of the highway for several miles and spot speeding or erratic drivers. Markings are placed on the highway at regular intervals so that speeds can be checked easily with a stop watch. Ground patrols, using radio-contact with the aircraft, then apprehend violators.

Other Speed Controls

The most frequently-used speed-control device is radar, an electronic instrument which can calculate the vehicle's speed with precise accuracy. An electronic signal is emitted, which reflects from an oncoming vehicle; the pattern shown by the reflected signal indicates the speed of the vehicle.

Electrical circuit-breakers are sometimes used to calculate the speed of a motor vehicle as it passes two points on the highway. A similar method is to calculate the speed as the vehicle crosses two lines similar to the lines which ring a bell as you enter a service station.

The advantages and disadvantages of these different methods lie in the accuracy, and the ease of setting up, maintaining, and operating, the apparatus. Radar is the most accurate.

The Breathalyzer

The methods of enforcement outlined above are to control the speeding driver. There is an even greater potential menace behind the wheel of a car, however, and that is the drinking driver. The operation of the breathalyzer as a means of controlling this problem was discussed in the previous chapter.

WHO ADMINISTERS THE LAW?

Since we have driving laws, and police officers to enforce these laws by apprehending violators, we must also have a method of judging if an apparent violator is actually guilty or not. Then, if he or she is found guilty, it is necessary to pass sentence by naming the penalty as prescribed within the bounds of the law. This duty is the function of our courts. The court systems and operations are described in the sections below.

The Crown Attorney

The Crown Attorney, who is named by the provincial Cabinet, presents the charge to the court, and represents the province or Crown in all such cases.

The Provincial Judges Court

The Provincial Judge named by the provincial cabinet hears the charge and statements from the Crown Attorney (or the appointed prosecutor) and his witnesses, as well as from the defence attorney and his witnesses. The judge weighs the evidence, and then passes judgement.

County Court

A driver found guilty in a Provincial Judges Court who feels the verdict or sentence was improper, may appeal the decision to the County Court, asking for either a lighter sentence or a new trial. The Crown, through its Crown Attorney, can also appeal a decision to this court.

The Supreme Court Of The Province

Decisions of the County Court can be appealed to the Supreme Court of the Province on points of law. Additional evidence cannot be introduced.

Appeal Court Of The Province

Appeals from the Supreme Court of a province go to the Appellate Division of the Supreme Court of the province.

The Supreme Court Of Canada

This court hears final appeals from all provinces and territories in Canada. The decisions of this court are final.

Court decisions may affect one's future. Legal advice and representation, therefore, are important in any court case.

PENALTIES FOR BREAKING THE LAW

The penalties for breaking the law – apart from the disastrous natural consequences of death, dismemberment, permanent disabilities, and financial loss – are fines, suspension of driving privileges, imprisonment, or a combination of any of these.

Fines

Fines are designed to hit the violator in the pocket book and thereby deter him from further violations of the law. Most statutes, by-laws, and regulations increase fines for more serious offences and for repeated violations.

Withdrawal Of Driving Privileges

Federal and provincial laws state that a driver's licence must be revoked if the driver is convicted of offences such as: criminal negligence in the operation of a motor vehicle, failing to stop at the scene of an accident, driving while ability is impaired by alcohol or drugs, and certain other violations.

In addition, some provinces have a demerit point system designed to identify traffic violators, and to protect pedestrians and careful motorists from drivers who abuse the privilege of operating motor vehicles. The aim of the point system is driver improvement. If an irresponsible driver fails to show improvement, he can be removed from the road.

If a driver is convicted of an offence or if he pays a fine out of court, points are recorded on the driver's record for the offences listed in the point-system table. Demerit points remain on the driver's record for a period of two years from the date of conviction. When the driver reaches approximately one-third of the maximum, he is urged to improve his driving habits. At two-thirds of the maximum, the driver may be required to attend a personal interview to discuss his record and give reasons why his licence should not be suspended. He will also be required to complete a driver re-examination, and should he fail to pass the test his licence will be cancelled.

If the driver reaches the maximum number of points his licence is suspended for a period varying from 30 days to 6 months, depending on the province he lives in. In some provinces, his licence will be reinstated at between one-third and two-thirds the maximum number of points, so that any additional points will immediately bring him to the interview level; if he should reach the maximum again, his licence will be suspended for a much longer period, such as six months. The point-system table can be found in your provincial Driver's Handbook.

Imprisonment

Federal and provincial laws provide that if a convicted person is unable to pay or refuses to pay a fine, he may be imprisoned for a period of time depending on the offence. For serious offences which are repeated, jail sentences may be handed down without the option of paying a fine as an alternative penalty. For very serious offences, a jail sentence may be mandatory even for a first conviction.

Laws are made for the protection of the individual in the community as well as for the efficient flow of traffic. It is the duty of every driver to obey all laws, for his own protection and the protection of others — not because of the penalties of law he may suffer.

17

insurance

The person who owns or drives a car without having appropriate insurance is extremely vulnerable. No matter who is driving his car, he is in danger of losing his possessions and much of his future income if an accident should occur. Dependence on his own skill or careful driving does not guarantee against human or mechanical error or future legal complications.

More than one car in ten in Canada is involved in a traffic accident each year. Another one hundred and fifty thousand are stolen or damaged by storms, fire, vandalism, or other causes. Therefore, when you purchase an automobile, there is one more important consideration which may be most important of all — *do not drive a car without proper insurance coverage.* This could be by far the most costly error you could make.

An accident may result in damage to someone else's property or in injury to a pedestrian, driver, or passenger. In many cases, driver's licences are revoked following accidents when there is no proof of financial responsibility such as insurance. This occurs *regardless of who was at fault*, and may apply for a fixed time, such as a year, or until the case is settled. Frequently a serious case will not be settled for a number of years, resulting in substantial expense, loss of time, and great mental anguish.

Your own car may be damaged or destroyed by fire, theft, vandals, wind or hailstorm, or by being involved in an accident. Although less serious than losing your possessions and even future income, it is still not pleasant to lose your car or be faced with substantial repair bills. Should this occur, you must make full payment of any sum that you may still owe for its purchase, even though the car may be completely destroyed.

Make no mistake — proper insurance coverage is essential.

CLASSES OF AUTOMOBILE INSURANCE

There are three general classifications of automobile insurance. The first, liability insurance, provides for injury or damage to others because of an accident in which the policy holder is legally responsible. The second, a combination of medical-payments insurance and accident-benefits insurance, is not based on legal liability; this coverage, which is compulsory in some areas, pays specified amounts to the driver and passengers in the insured car, and to members of the immediate family of the car owner. The third type, physical damage insurance, reimburses a car owner for damage to his own automobile.

Third Party Liability Insurance

From the point of view of personal responsibility and consequences, the type of accident that injures another person or damages another's property is the most serious. The type of insurance which protects you against claims for injury or damage to others is known as *liability insurance*. This protects you against all claims made against you, up to the amounts set forth in the policy. Liability insurance pays you no money, but it protects you against other persons' claims resulting from an automobile accident.

In addition to paying for your negligence up to the specified amount, your insurance company will pay your legal costs and any court costs which may be involved if you are sued as the result of an accident.

The *minimum limits* of liability insurance vary from $35,000 to $50,000 in most provinces. However, these limits are not always sufficient to pay for all liability claims. Coverage up to a higher limit is generally available at a comparatively small cost.

Accident Benefits And Medical Payments

ACCIDENT-BENEFITS COVERAGE

In some provinces accident-benefits coverage is compulsory; in other provinces, this coverage is available for only a few dollars a year. Accident-benefits coverage provides weekly indemnity for employed persons, as well as stipulated death or dismemberment benefits and additional coverages *without regard to fault*. These benefits apply to anyone in the car, any member of the family while in someone else's car, and to pedestrians.

MEDICAL-PAYMENTS INSURANCE

Benefits under medical-payments insurance are also paid without regard to fault. While most people in Canada now have government hospital and medical coverage, these benefits will provide extra coverage in some cases. For example, they will pay for dental work or the extra cost of semi-private hospital accomodation if you are hurt in an accident. There is a maximum limit to payments, usually $2,000 for each individual, but many companies will provide higher limits for an additional premium.

Types of Physical Damage Insurance

Another general class of automobile insurance covers the car owner for his own personal loss. In this class we find three types of coverage.

COMPREHENSIVE

This coverage pays you if your car is damaged or destroyed as a result of fire, explosion, windstorm, hurricane, tornado, hail, water and flood, earthquake, falling objects, theft and robbery, missiles, vandalism, riot and civil commotion, or broken glass. It will also reimburse you, under certain circumstances, for renting a car if yours is stolen. Comprehensive coverage, however, does not pay any of the costs incurred through damage in a collision.

COLLISION

This type of coverage pays you for accidental damage to your car whether or not the accident is your fault. The main purpose of collision insurance is to avoid a large loss which the insured person cannot afford, such as total destruction of the car. Since the majority of persons can afford a small loss, this coverage is generally written with a "deductible" provision, such as "$100.00 deductible." The higher the deductible amount, the lower the cost of the insurance. The deductible provision requires that you pay the deductible amount, say the first $100.00, towards repair or replacement of your car, and the insurance company pays the balance.

ALL-PERILS

All-Perils coverage is a combination of comprehensive and collision insurance.

GOVERNMENT CAR INSURANCE

Some provinces now have a car insurance plan that is operated by the provincial governments. Details of rates of insurance and the regulations relating to this type of insurance can be obtained from the provinces where this scheme is in operation.

CONDITIONS THAT AFFECT INSURANCE COST

When you buy an insurance policy, you are buying protection. For this protection you pay the company a fee, called a premium. The premium you pay is based upon a number of factors:
1. The type of insurance bought.
2. The amount of coverage you bought.
3. The type of car you own.
4. Where you live.
5. How the car is used (that is, whether for business or for pleasure).
6. Your driving record.
7. Whether a youthful driver, generally under the age of 25, will drive the car, and whether he has taken an approved high school driver education course.

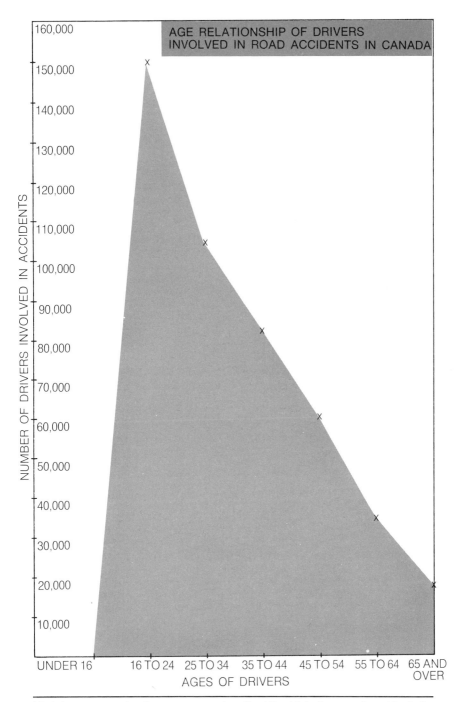

AGE RELATIONSHIP OF DRIVERS
INVOLVED IN ROAD ACCIDENTS IN CANADA

NUMBER OF DRIVERS INVOLVED IN ACCIDENTS

160,000
150,000
140,000
130,000
120,000
110,000
100,000
90,000
80,000
70,000
60,000
50,000
40,000
30,000
20,000
10,000

UNDER 16   16 TO 24   25 TO 34   35 TO 44   45 TO 54   55 TO 64   65 AND OVER

AGES OF DRIVERS

High insurance rates for young people reflect the high degree of accidents for the age group

In many cases girls under age 25 can drive the family car without any change in rate providing they are not the principal operators. For a young man under 25 years, there is a surcharge which is 50 to 75 per cent of the premium already paid.

If a young man owns his own car, or if he is the principal operator of a car, his rates will be substantially higher than those paid by a more mature driver. The rates decline as the driver becomes older, since most companies charge the most to insure 16, 17, and 18 year old male principal operators. If he keeps a clear driving record his premium may drop. However, if his record is not clear, his insurance may be subject to a surcharge or the company may elect to provide only the minimum cover.

The major cost of insurance premiums is determined by the traffic-accident experience of all persons insured in a given area. If the number of claims paid for accidents increases, the insurance companies must pay out additional sums of money, and automobile insurance costs go up. Most companies reduce premiums of drivers who have had accident-free driving records for a specified number of years.

Married men under 25 and girls who own their own cars pay higher premiums than drivers over 25, but much lower premiums than those charged to young unmarried men.

Many companies recognize that high school students who have taken driver education courses have shown their willingness to accept the responsibility to become safe and competent drivers. The result is that they charge a lower premium for occasional male drivers under 25 and all principal drivers or owners under 25 who have completed an approved driver education course.

Insurance rates vary from company to company. Competition between companies is keen. You may find that you can get a lower rate if you check with several agents or company representatives.

DRIVING SOMEONE ELSE'S CAR

If a car is insured, the insurance is effective no matter who is driving, provided that the driver has the owner's permission, is qualified to drive, and is not impaired by alcohol or drugs.

If you own your own car, you have additional protection in that your liability insurance "follows" you, under most circumstances, when you drive another car. Your liability insurance in such cases is "excess" insurance over and above the liability insurance carried by the owner

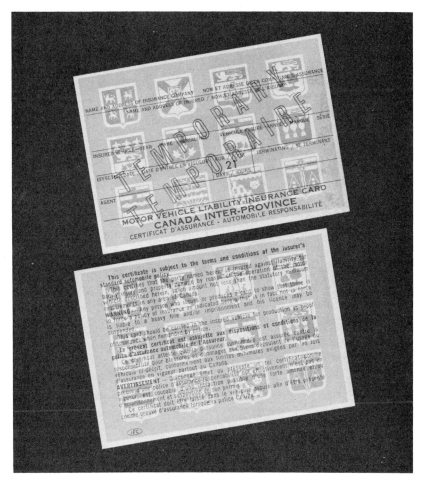

An inter-province liability insurance card. It provides proof of the insurance, name of the insured, and description of the insured vehicle. It should be carried at all times in the vehicle

of the car. Liability insurance on your parents' car does not follow you, but medical-benefits and accident-benefits coverage does, provided that you live at home. Collision insurance does not follow you, since this coverage is for the car, not the driver.

If you don't own your own car and you drive other people's cars regularly — and you aren't sure if they are insured or not — you might find it worthwhile to have a "driver's policy." The rates for a driver's policy are about the same as you would pay if you owned your own car.

MOTOR VEHICLE ACCIDENT CLAIMS FUND

Some provincial governments have designed a Motor Vehicle Accident Claims Fund, which protects innocent persons and their property against uninsured motorists.

While the percentage of uninsured motorists is small, there are also non-resident motorists who might not be insured, and also hit-and-run drivers, all of whom create the problems which this Fund is designed to protect you against.

The Fund is usually supported by charging an extra fee to the uninsured car-owner when a vehicle licence is purchased.

By choosing not to carry liability insurance, a driver has stacked up terrifying odds against himself. **Even though he has paid the extra money for the privilege of driving his car on the roads, he is still not protected**. The Uninsured Motor Vehicle Fee is not a form of Government insurance that permits uninsured drivers to escape their responsibilities.

When requested by a police constable or authorized officer, you must be able to produce either proof that the vehicle is insured under a liability policy for bodily injury and property damage, or else a receipt for payment of the Uninsured Motor Vehicle Fee. If you are at fault in an accident and you do not pay for damages, your driving privileges will be suspended, and you cannot be reinstated until you do the following:

1. Pay back the Fund.
2. File proof of financial responsibility.

Court awards of $10,000, $20,000, or $30,000 are not uncommon. If you do not have liability insurance coverage, your savings, your home, and your future income are all in danger. You may have to make monthly payments for the rest of your life. The Motor Vehicle Accident Claims Fund is authorized to pay up to $50,000 in Ontario, exclusive of costs, to the victims of uninsured drivers — and you will be obliged to repay every cent of this to the Fund if you are at fault.

Why risk financial ruin when liability insurance is available?

18

how the wheels move

The modern automobile is made up of over twenty thousand parts, engineered to fit and operate dependably together for efficient and safe operation — if properly treated and cared for. One does not need to be an automotive technician to drive a car safely, but a basic understanding of the major components and their capabilities and required care can save you money and also prevent unnecessary and expensive breakdowns. A general knowledge will help you understand the reasons why engine oil must be the proper grade and changed frequently; why spark plugs are necessary, what they do, and why they need attention periodically; and other basic points of operating your car. Answers to questions such as, what happens to the gas I put in the tank? how does pushing on the accelerator make the car speed up? what stops the wheels from turning when I put the brakes on? These are only a few of the questions you can answer when a very simple study is made of the automobile. With a little knowledge of the vehicle, you will know what a mechanic is talking about when he recommends that certain repairs need to be made on your car.

The automobile is made up of two major parts, the body and the chassis.

The body of the car is what a person sees. It consists of the roof, doors, fenders, hood, trunk, interior seats and upholstery, chrome mouldings, and glass. It provides comfort for the driver and passengers, and protects them from the elements and from collision.

The chassis of the car consists of the power train and all necessary parts to control and suspend the entire automobile. It is this part of the car which we will be primarily concerned with.

The chassis may be divided into five different groups for easier study. These will be discussed below.

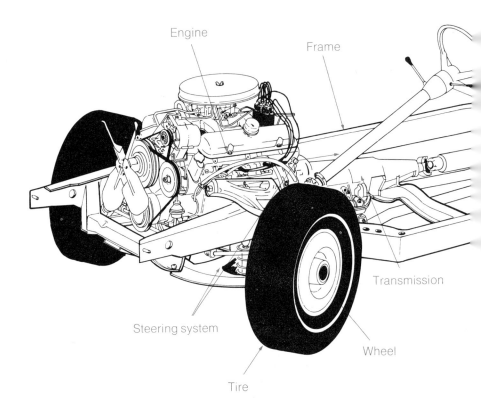

Engine

Frame

Transmission

Steering system

Wheel

Tire

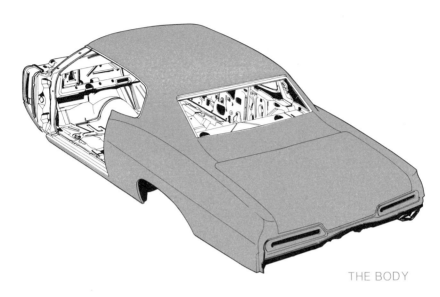

THE BODY

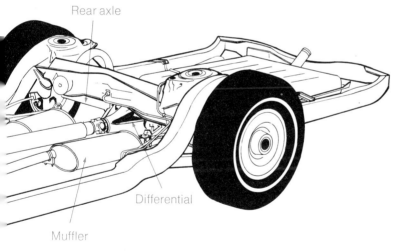

Rear axle

Differential

Muffler

shaft

THE CHASSIS

THE RUNNING GEAR

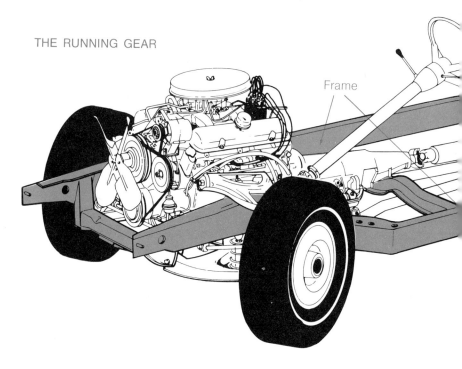

Frame

THE RUNNING GEAR

The running gear consists of those parts of the car which suspend the entire automobile. The main part is the frame, which consists of two heavy steel rails which run parallel to each other the entire length of the car. These two rails are held in alignment and are strengthened by crossmembers, which also serve as points to which all other parts attach either directly or indirectly.

The wheels, tires, and suspension parts hold the frame assembly from the road. The suspension consists of springs (or on some cars, torsion bars) and shock absorbers, connected by suitable control-arms and linkages to the frame. When a wheel encounters an irregularity in the road surface (a bump or hole), that wheel can independently move over or in-and-out of the hole without the entire car changing its relative position. The spring will compress and release, allowing only the wheel to move. The shocks control the oscillations of the springs; without them, the car would bounce almost continuously.

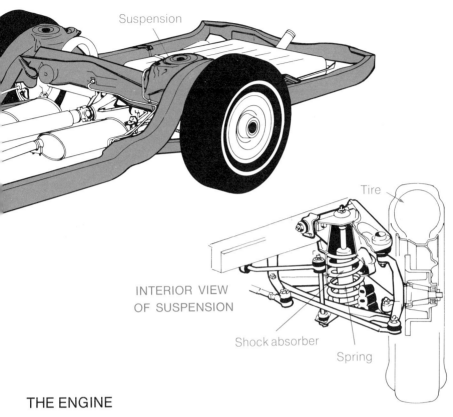

Suspension

Tire

INTERIOR VIEW
OF SUSPENSION

Shock absorber

Spring

THE ENGINE

The engine consists of a number of mechanical parts and the auxiliary systems which are necessary for its operation. Different types of engines may have various special features of their own, but the fundamental principles are shared by nearly all automobile power-plants. The only exception is the Wankel engine, now being used in certain European and Japanese cars, which is totally different from the familiar piston engine.

The engine cylinder-block is the main body of the engine. It is usually made of cast iron and steel, or aluminum. Several large smooth holes are bored in the block, called cylinders.

Depending on the engine, there may be four, six, or eight cylinders. An engine with eight cylinders usually has two rows of four cylinders arranged in a "V shape;" this is called a "V-8 engine."

A cylinder head fits on top of the cylinder block; this unit contains the combustion chamber, valves, and the spark-plug holes.

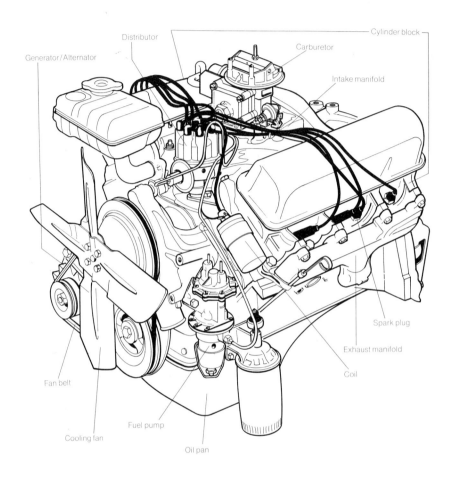

Distributor
Carburetor
Cylinder block
Generator/Alternator
Intake manifold
Spark plug
Exhaust manifold
Coil
Fan belt
Fuel pump
Cooling fan
Oil pan

V-8 ENGINE

Inside each cylinder is an aluminum piston which moves up and down. The piston has rings on it which make a seal against the inner surface of the cylinder, so that compression cannot leak past. If the piston-rings are worn, the engine will lose power and will also use excessive quantities of oil.

A connecting rod joins the piston to the crankshaft, which is

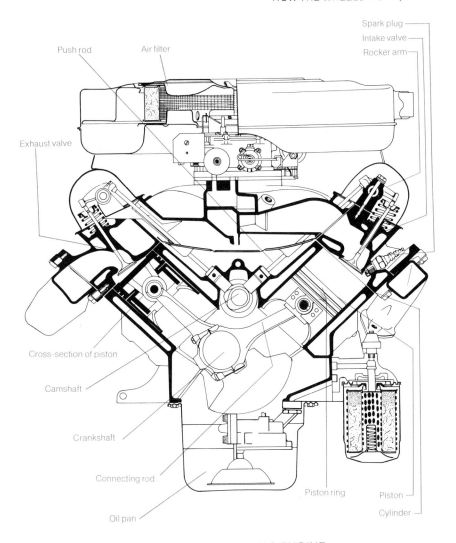

Spark plug

Intake valve

Push rod   Air filter   Rocker arm

Exhaust valve

Cross-section of piston

Camshaft

Crankshaft

Connecting rod

Piston ring   Piston

Oil pan   Cylinder

CROSS-SECTION OF V-8 ENGINE

located in the lower part of the cylinder block. The purpose of the connecting rod and crankshaft is to change the up-and-down motion of the piston to rotary motion. This is necessary because only rotary motion can be transmitted through the power train to the wheels.

An oil pan is bolted to the bottom of the cylinder block to act as a reservoir for oil to lubricate the moving parts.

Since this is an internal-combustion engine, fuel and air mixed as a vapour enters the combustion chamber and cylinder, is ignited and burned, and then expelled. Valves are required to open a port or passageway for fuel and air to enter. These are called intake valves. Exhaust valves open a port to let the burnt gases out. Each cylinder in an engine must have one intake valve and one exhaust valve.

The valves must be opened and closed at the proper time. A camshaft is driven at one-half the speed of the crankshaft by a pair of timing gears. The camshaft has cams or lobes on it, one for each valve. As the camshaft turns, the lobes press upwards on a push rod, which in turn presses against a rocker arm, which then pushes against the valve, forcing it to open.

When the cam turns further, a valve spring closes the valve. Some engines have the camshaft in the lower part of the engine, beside the crankcase, while others have it above the cylinder head; in the latter type, the camshaft often operates the valves directly, so that push rods are not needed.

The Four-Stroke Cycle

The "four-stroke cycle" of engine operation is a very simple series of events which repeat very rapidly so long as the engine is running. A "stroke" is the movement of a piston from the top of the cylinder to the bottom of the cylinder or vice versa.

To start the engine, the electric starting-motor turns the crankshaft, and the piston moves down from the top of the cylinder. The first phase of the cycle, called the intake stroke, now begins. The intake valve is opened and the vacuum created above the piston as it descends causes a fuel-vapour and air mixture to be drawn into the cylinder from the carburetor. (The operation of the carburetor is discussed in this chapter, on page 194.) When the piston reaches the bottom of its stroke, the intake valve closes.

With both valves closed, the piston starts the second stroke travelling upwards, and the fuel-and-air mixture is compressed into a tiny volume at the top of the cylinder. This is the compression stroke.

As the piston nears the top of its compression stroke, a surge of high-voltage current (as much as 30,000 volts) bridges the gap at the spark plug, and ignites the fuel and air. It is this burning process that produces the heat energy to drive the pistons down with a force of as much as seven tons pressure. This is the power stroke.

THE FOUR-STROKE CYCLE

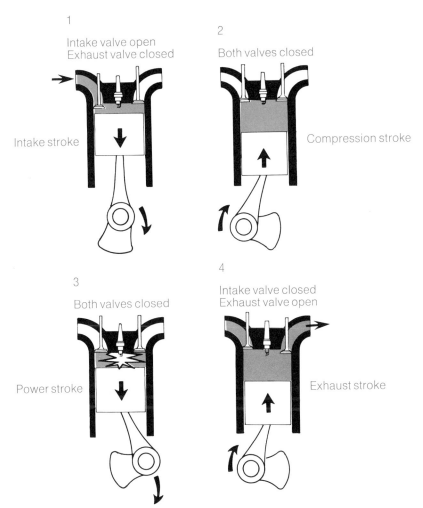

1

Intake valve open
Exhaust valve closed

Intake stroke

2

Both valves closed

Compression stroke

3

Both valves closed

Power stroke

4

Intake valve closed
Exhaust valve open

Exhaust stroke

The four strokes comprise one complete cycle of a single cylinder. Each four-stroke cycle is followed by another and another in a continuous process in each cylinder of the engine. In turn, each piston transmits the power to the crankshaft.

As the energy from the power stroke forces the piston down, the crankshaft and flywheel gain enough momentum to carry through to the next phase of the cycle, the exhaust stroke. After the fuel and air mixture has been burned, it must be expelled. The exhaust valve opens and the piston moves up again, pushing the burnt gases out the exhaust port, and through the exhaust manifold and exhaust pipe into the muffler, where the noise is silenced. Finally, the exhaust gases pass through the tailpipe and into the atmosphere.

It should be remembered, of course, that the above explanation of the four-stroke cycle dealt with only one cylinder, whereas in an actual engine, the same process is taking place in many cylinders in rapid succession. In a V-8 engine, about 12,000 complete cycles occur every minute when the car is travelling at 70 miles per hour.

The Cooling System

The internal-combustion engine produces great quantities of heat which must be either used or dissipated. About one-third of the heat energy of the fuel is changed into useful mechanical energy. Another one-third of the heat goes out the exhaust system. The remaining one-third is absorbed by the engine parts, which therefore must be cooled. The cooling system of the automobile serves three purposes. First, it prevents overheating, which could result in serious damage to the engine. Second, it keeps the engine at whatever temperature is most efficient for its operation. Third, it supplies heat for the passenger compartment and for the defroster.

Surrounding the engine cylinder and head is a channel or water jacket which is filled with water (or water and anti-freeze solution to prevent freezing in the winter). The water absorbs some of the heat caused by the burning fuel and the friction of the moving parts. A thermostat is located near the top of the engine to control the minimum operating temperature of the engine. When the temperature of the coolant reaches approximately 180 degrees Fahrenheit, the thermostat opens and the water goes through a hose to the top of the radiator. A fan draws cool air through the radiator to cool the water from the motor. When the water is cooled, it leaves the radiator through a lower outlet-hose to the water pump, which helps circulate the water through the cooling system.

The radiator has a cap on it to prevent evaporation of the coolant and to increase the pressure within the cooling system in order to raise the boiling point of the water. Care must be exercised when removing this cap. Use a folded cloth to prevent scalding your hand. Turn it slowly in a counter-clockwise direction to the first notch; do not turn further until all the pressure has been released. Failure to observe this simple precaution may result in serious scalding.

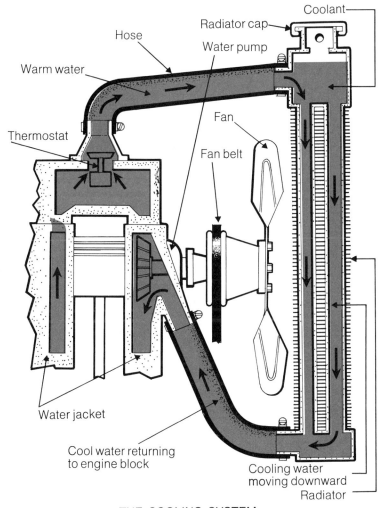

THE COOLING SYSTEM

THE FUEL SYSTEM

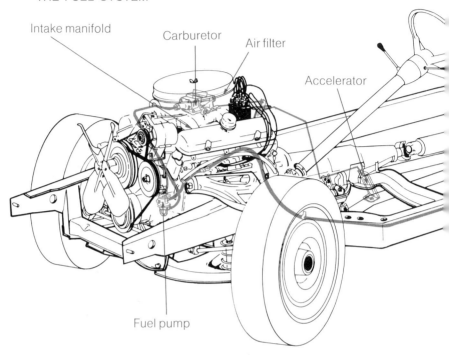

Intake manifold

Carburetor

Air filter

Accelerator

Fuel pump

The Fuel System

The fuel system of the automobile consists of three major parts: the fuel tank, the fuel pump, and the carburetor. The fuel tank, which is usually located at the back of the car, is connected to the fuel pump and carburetor by steel tubes called the fuel lines. The fuel pump delivers gasoline from the tank to the carburetor, with the rate of flow being governed by the engine's demand.

The carburetor has three basic functions. It must vapourize the fuel, mix it with the proper amount of air, and deliver this mixture through the intake manifold to all the cylinders. The amount of fuel and air delivered varies with engine speed and load.

The carburetor is basically a simple device, although it is precision-made and must be accurately adjusted to function properly. A float bowl holds a small quantity of fuel at all times, which can be rapidly delivered to the engine to meet any sudden demand for power. A hollow tube or tubes, called "barrels," provide a passageway for air. When the engine operates, air enters through an air filter

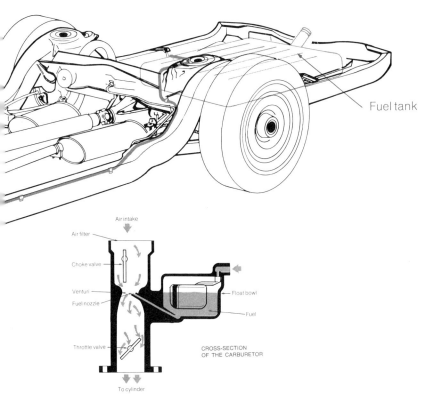

Fuel tank

Air intake

Air filter

Choke valve

Venturi

Fuel nozzle

Float bowl

Fuel

Throttle valve

CROSS-SECTION
OF THE CARBURETOR

To cylinder

on top of the carburetor, so that any harmful dirt can be removed. The air is then drawn down the hollow tube of the carburetor past a narrow passage called a venturi. This produces a vacuum, which causes fuel to flow from a calibrated nozzle. The fuel-and-air mixture then passes a valve in the bottom of the carburetor called a throttle valve, which is connected to the accelerator pedal in the passenger compartment. When the driver presses on the accelerator the throttle valve is opened, so that more air and fuel can enter the cylinders, thereby increasing engine power and speed.

When the engine is cold, a richer mixture (more fuel and less air) is required. A choke valve at the top of the carburetor automatically closes when the accelerator is depressed for cold starts. This cuts off some of the air. As the engine warms to normal operating tempera-ture, the choke opens gradually. Some cars have a manual choke, which must be closed when starting a cold engine and opened gradually as it warms up.

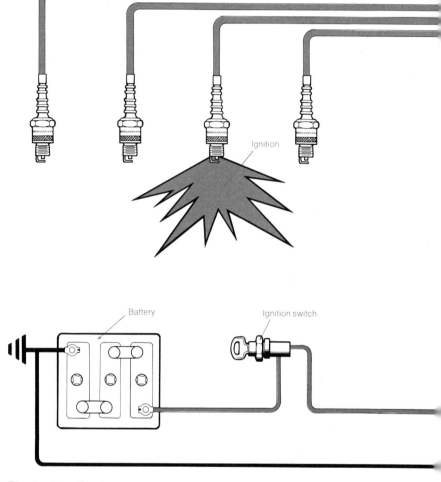

The Ignition System

The ignition system has two basic functions. The first is to increase the voltage from the battery of the car. The battery has sufficient voltage to operate the starter, lights, and other accessories, but not enough to fire the spark plugs. The voltage required for this operation ranges from 7,000 to 30,000 volts, depending on the type of engine, the speed and load of the engine, and the condition of the spark plugs.

The second function of the ignition system is to fire the spark plugs at exactly the right time and in the proper order. This is done

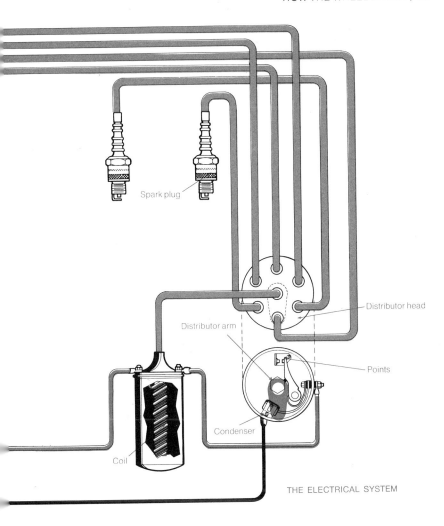

Spark plug

Distributor head

Distributor arm

Points

Condenser

Coil

THE ELECTRICAL SYSTEM

with a distributor, which has a set of automatic switches called points or contacts, which open and close once for each cylinder with every other revolution.

In an eight-cylinder engine, the spark plugs each produce about 15 million sparks in 10,000 miles of driving, and the ignition points open and close about 120 million times. It is wise, therefore, to replace these parts at about 10,000 miles to maintain good engine efficiency and performance.

The Lubrication System

The moving parts in the engine must be lubricated to reduce friction, heat, and wear. The oil pan at the bottom of the engine stores the oil, and the oil pump forces the oil through filters and tiny holes leading to all moving parts to assure proper lubrication. Failure to lubricate the engine may result in immediate destruction of the entire unit. The oil light or oil-pressure gauge on the dashboard will indicate if the lubrication system is functioning. These do not tell how much oil is in the engine, however; an oil-level dipstick is located under the hood for this purpose. If the oil light comes on while the engine is running or if the oil-pressure gauge reads near zero, stop the engine immediately and get a mechanic to check it. It will probably just be low on oil, but the possibility always exists that a more serious fault may be the problem.

When selecting oil for your car, choose according to climate and driving conditions. The "viscosity rating" is one guide you can use to know which oil to buy. The lower the viscosity rating, the more easily the oil will flow, especially at low temperatures. Therefore, number 5 or 10 oil should be used during the winter months for easy starting and improved initial lubrication when the engine is cold. However, low-viscosity oil loses its lubricating properties when it gets very hot; therefore, a thicker oil, such as number 30, is ideal during the summer months. A number 20 oil is suitable during the spring and fall. Most oil companies have a multi-viscosity oil such as "10-W-30," which has a viscosity of 10 at low temperatures and 30 at high temperatures. This type of oil may be used throughout the year.

Oil must withstand very high temperatures and pressures, and must also clean as it lubricates. Detergents in modern oil aid in this process. The oil's ability to resist deterioration determines its "service rating." In turn, the type of driving you do determines the service rating of the oil your engine needs. Check the oil you buy — the grade should be indicated on the can; if it isn't — beware of the quality.

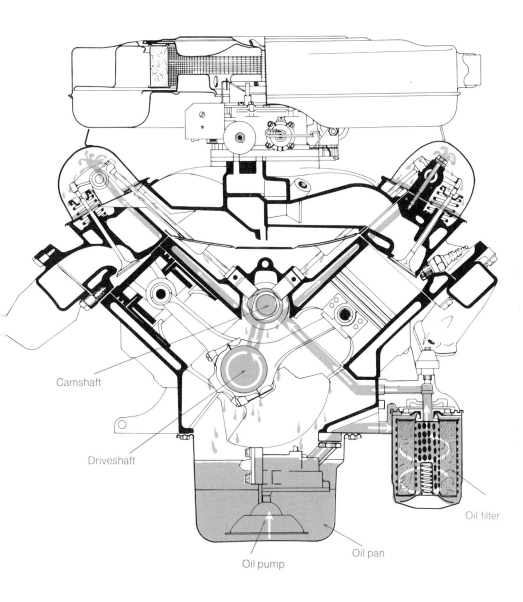

Camshaft

Driveshaft

Oil filter

Oil pan

Oil pump

THE LUBRICATION SYSTEM

THE POWER TRAIN

The power the engine develops must be transmitted by a number of mechanical units called, collectively, the power train. In most cars, the engine is in the front and the rear wheels do the driving. Cars with a different engine-to-drive set-up will have a different power train, but most of the basic essentials are similar.

The Automatic Transmission

Most cars today are equipped with an automatic transmission. The other type of transmission, the manually-operated gearshift, is also popular, especially in imported cars; since this unit is basically different from the automatic, it will be discussed in a separate chapter (Chapter 21).

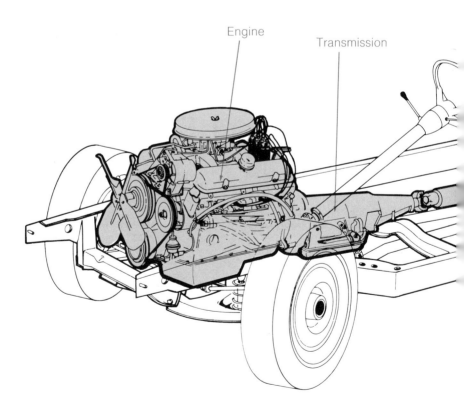

Engine

Transmission

The automatic transmission is basically a "fluid coupling" connecting the rear of the engine crankshaft to the driveshaft. The coupling consists of two sets of turbine-like blades inside a tightly-sealed housing. One set of blades is connected to the engine, and the other set to the gears in the transmission. There is no direct mechanical connection between the two sets of blades themselves; instead, the housing is filled with automatic-transmission fluid, which is a special oil. As the engine turns one turbine, the oil is directed against the other turbine's blades with a great force, causing it to rotate. This movement of the second turbine then turns a series of gears in the transmission. As the car moves, the gear-ratios will automatically change according to the hydraulic oil-pressure, the car's speed, load conditions, and acceleration.

When idling the car in gear, "slippage" occurs in the fluid

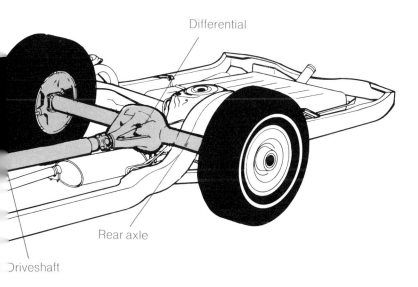

Differential

Rear axle

Driveshaft

THE POWER TRAIN

coupling (that is, the second turbine slips, instead of turning with the first), but the car may still tend to "creep" forward very slowly. It is therefore suggested that when stopping a car momentarily in Drive or Reverse, the brake pedal should be held on to keep the car stationary.

When the transmission is put in Park, the rear wheels and drive shaft are locked but the engine can still run and be started. The locking device is a small pin that locks a gear to the transmission case. It is recommended that the parking brake be applied first before moving the selector lever to Park. This takes the strain off this pin; if someone bumps your car when it is in Park, serious damage could otherwise result.

Neutral gear is used for starting (as well as Park), and also for idling the engine with no power flow in the automatic transmission. Since the car is free to roll when in Neutral, be sure the parking brake is on. The engine should not start in Drive, Low, or Reverse; if it does, it should be fixed immediately. Low gear is used for pulling heavy loads at slow speeds, for starting up hills, or for increased engine-braking when descending long steep hills. When kept in low gear, the transmission cannot shift to high gear by itself.

The Driveshaft Or Propellor Shaft

The driveshaft is a long tube which transfers the rotating motion from the transmission to the differential. At either end of the driveshaft is a universal joint; this joint allows the driveshaft to move whenever the rear wheel hits a bump without interrupting the transfer of power.

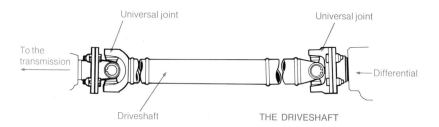

Universal joint

Universal joint

To the transmission

Differential

Driveshaft

THE DRIVESHAFT

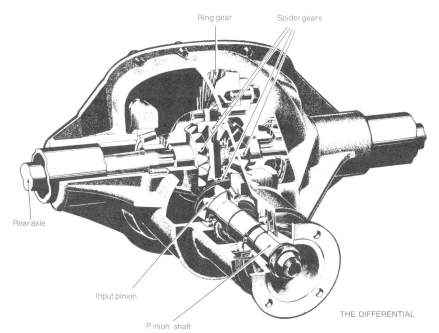

Ring gear   Spider gears

Rear axle

Input pinion

Pinion shaft

THE DIFFERENTIAL

The Differential

The differential has three principal functions. First, it must transmit the powerflow through an angle of 90 degrees from the driveshaft to the rear axle. Second, it makes possible another gear reduction of about three or four-to-one, which enables the engine to operate within its most efficient range of speeds. The third function of the differential is to enable the rear wheels to go around a corner smoothly. When turning, the outside wheel must go a greater distance than the inside wheel. To accomplish this, each wheel must have a separate axle; the "inter-relationship" of the two axles is achieved by four bevel spider gears driven by the input pinion and ring gear within the differential (see illustration).

If one rear wheel is on ice and the other wheel is on pavement, the effect of the differential can cause the wheel on ice to spin, while the wheel on the pavement will not turn at all — with the net result that the car does not move. This problem can be overcome by specifying a "positive-traction" differential when ordering a new car. Differentials of this type are more complicated and expensive, but they do succeed in transmitting power to both wheels even if one wheel is on ice.

THE CONTROL SYSTEM

Steering

The driver controls the direction of the car by turning the steering wheel. The steering wheel is connected to the front wheels of the car by the steering linkage. This is done in such a way that one wheel turns sharper than the other when rounding a corner. The front wheels themselves pivot on individual ball joints in the front suspension. The steering linkage also acts as a gear reduction system with a ratio of about 20-to-1, so that less effort is required for turning.

The front wheels are not exactly vertical, but are tilted in or out at the top, and back or forward from the side, in order to aid steering and vehicle stability. Front-end alignment angles are adjustable and need checking occasionally.

Power steering helps turn the wheels with much less effort on the part of the driver. A hydraulic pump driven by a belt provides the power assist. If the power assist fails, steering is still possible, but the effort is much greater than that required even for standard steering.

THE BRAKING SYSTEM

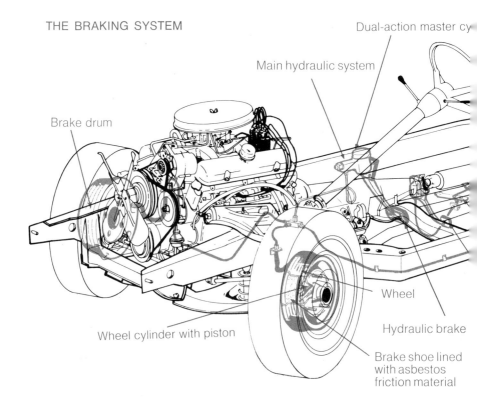

Dual-action master cy

Main hydraulic system

Brake drum

Wheel

Wheel cylinder with piston

Hydraulic brake

Brake shoe lined with asbestos friction material

The Braking System

If the car will go, it must also be able to stop. All modern cars have two braking systems, the main hydraulic system, and the mechanical parking-brake system which may also be used in an emergency.

When you step on the brake pedal, a rod moves a piston in a master hydraulic cylinder, which forces hydraulic fluid through a system of tubes to four separate cylinders located one at each wheel. Also fastened to each wheel is a steel brake drum, within which is a pair of brake-shoes, lined with an asbestos friction material. The cylinders at the wheels each have two pistons in them, which are forced by hydraulic pressure to press the brake lining against the rotating drum. The friction between the drum and the lining causes the wheel to slow down or stop. When the brake pedal is released, springs pull the brake shoes back, and the displaced fluid returns through the hydraulic fluid lines to the master cylinder.

The greater the speed of the drum and wheel, the more friction is necessary to stop the car. Friction generates heat, and if too much heat is created, the brakes fail. A failure of this nature is called "brake fade." This is the reason why low gear must be used when descending long or steep hills and mountains. The engine acts as a

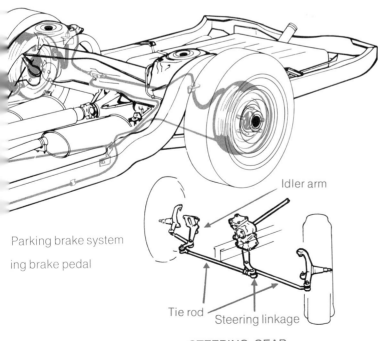

Idler arm

Parking brake system

ing brake pedal

Tie rod

Steering linkage

STEERING GEAR

brake to help reduce the work the brakes must do, thereby reducing the possibility of brake fade.

Some cars have "disc brakes," which are basically callipers that press against a rotating disc fastened to the wheel. Disc brakes have a greater ability to dissipate heat, and therefore are less likely to suffer from brake fade.

Brakes are not efficient when wet. When travelling on a wet road or after driving through a puddle or a flooded area, be sure to test the brakes. If they are not working properly, holding the brake on for several moments while you drive will quickly dry them out.

Power brakes require less effort on behalf of the driver but *do not* reduce the braking distance.

The parking brake operates by two cables connected to a lever or pedal assembly. The cable operates the same brake shoes as the hydraulic system, but on the rear wheels only. The parking brake, however, will stay on when the car is parked (unlike the hydraulic brake), and can also be used in the event of a hydraulic failure. If you use the parking brake to stop in an emergency, pull and hold out the parking brake release and use the parking brake pedal with a pumping action to avoid skidding.

THE ELECTRICAL SYSTEM

The modern automobile depends upon electrical energy to perform many duties. Electricity supplies power for starting the car, for lighting, for the ignition, and for operating many of the accessories.

The battery is the main source of electrical energy. Like any storage device, however, if the battery is continually drained it will soon run out of potential. To keep it at full power, a generator or alternator is used to recharge it.

The alternator, which is driven by the fan belt, changes mechanical energy into electrical energy. It supplies current to the electrical system whenever the engine is running. The alternator is a fairly new invention; many older cars have a generator, which performs the same functions, but generally is less efficient.

A voltage regulator controls the maximum alternator-output to prevent the battery from being overcharged, to protect the alternator from burning itself out, and to protect the other electrical equipment from too high a voltage.

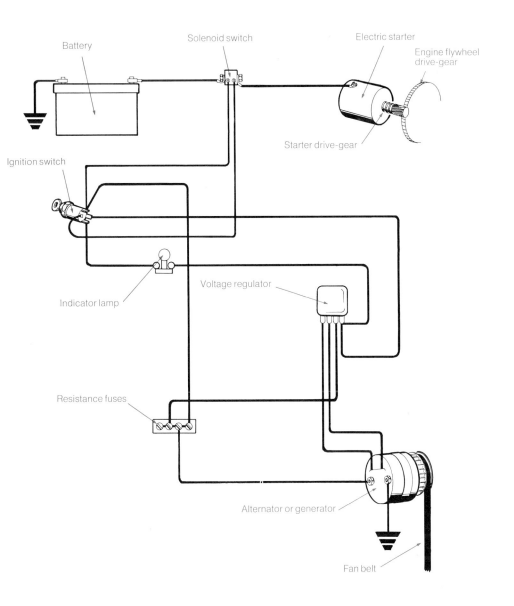

THE ELECTRICAL SYSTEM

If the alternator light comes on when the engine is operating or if the ammeter indicates a discharge, the charging circuit is not functioning properly, and the battery will soon go dead. Take the car immediately to a mechanic for repairs. The most likely cause is a loose or broken fan belt, which is easy and inexpensive to repair.

The starting circuit consists of the battery, a solenoid switch, a powerful electric motor, and a starter drive mechanism. When the key is turned to the "start" position, the solenoid switch sends battery current to the starter and the ignition system. The starter drive-gear cranks the engine by a large gear on the engine flywheel until the engine starts. The electric starter will disengage automatically at this point, provided that the key is not held in the start position.

If an engine is difficult to start, never use the starter for more than 30 seconds continuously or it will burn itself out. Allow it to stand for about half a minute between cranking periods to cool off.

Many accessories are operated electrically, such as power seats, power windows, radio and tape decks, power antennae, lights, cigar lighters, clocks, and a host of others. These items place an additional load on the battery. It is essential, therefore, to have the battery properly serviced and the charging circuit kept in good condition.

Do all these technical details leave you more than a little bit confused? Don't worry about that — unless you have a natural mechanical aptitude, no one would expect you to understand the inner workings of the automobile on the basis of one quick chapter such as this one. You may wonder why you should even be concerned with the mechanical side of your car, especially if you plan to have a professional mechanic do the work anyway. There are several good reasons why any driver should have a rudimentary knowledge of how his car functions, however. For one thing, this knowledge enables you to look for and notice any irregularities in the way the car runs, and to deduce whether or not these irregularities mean that a future problem may be developing. By this means, trouble spots can be caught before they become too serious. And even though you might not plan to repair your own car, if you can knowledgeably describe the symptoms to a mechanic, he will probably figure out the problem more quickly, thereby saving you some money on his bill. All in all, even a little knowledge of how your car runs will save you money and increase your driving pleasure at the same time.

19

buying your own car

Before you buy a car, you must be aware of the responsibilities that will be yours. The initial cost of the car is usually the only consideration one thinks about — but this is one of the most misleading concepts that could be imagined. Next to buying a home, a car is probably the biggest investment you will make, not just for the initial cost, but for the up-keep as well, which is almost as expensive.

Perhaps your main objective when you begin to drive is to own your personal car. This is a perfectly normal wish, but you must be willing to accept the responsibility involved. Where will you get the money to buy and operate the car? Where will you drive it? When will you drive it? Who accepts the financial and moral responsibility for you and your actions? Admittedly these are not very glamorous questions, but they are·unavoidable, and should be given a great deal of thought before you make the decision to go ahead.

The student who attends school regularly and has a part-time job has enough to do. When the same student buys a car, he may be taking on too heavy a burden of additional problems. A study has showed that a "B" student who buys a car will almost definitely drop a grade in scholastic achievement. He will probably spend more time driving — and repairing — the car than he previously spent walking when he did not have a car to think about. He must continue to work to pay for the gas, oil, tires, licence, insurance, etc., which are absolutely necessary to operate it. He will get more out of his life socially, but because he is going more places he is spending more money.

Try figuring out the costs of driving. The average driver will go about 12,000 miles a year, at an average overall cost of 10 cents per mile (this is the average cost-per-mile of driving in Canada, calculated on the basis of extensive nation-wide surveys). This works out to $1,200.00 per year to operate a car. While some may get by with a lower figure, for others the cost often works out to be more. If

you buy a very inexpensive worn-out car, you may find that the previous owner knew exactly what he was doing when he unloaded it. Don't buy somebody else's troubles — you may learn about the costs of owning a car more quickly than you expected.

Another point to consider when you as a minor purchase a car. If you get into a serious accident for which you are judged at fault, and liability is not covered entirely by insurance, your parents may be financially responsible. It would be nothing less than tragic to bring financial ruin to one's parents because of a moment of carelessness or inattention.

BUYING A NEW CAR

Everyone would like to buy a new car, but not everyone can afford it. A new car will give longer service with less trouble, and you can buy any model you wish with the equipment you want. Warranties to protect your investment are much better on new cars, and a new car will most likely enhance your social status. However, one must realize that buying a new car is a heavy financial load, and could possibly be a greater burden than you could cope with.

Before you buy a new car, set a financial ceiling for yourself. If you do not have ready cash, and most people don't, work out a monthly payment maximum you can afford, and don't go over 36 months to complete the payments. Remember you will have operating costs at 10 cents per mile while you drive, and even though a portion of these costs will be taken care of by your monthly payments, you will still have the regular expenses of gas, lubrication, and incidentals.

Before you choose which car you want, establish in your own mind the kind of driving you will be doing. If you drive mostly in the city, either a small car or a compact is your best buy for economy and manoeuverability. If you intend to travel long distances, on the other hand, a full-sized car is more comfortable. Try to decide on the model or size of car, and the equipment you want, such as size of motor, type of transmission, power equipment, and comfort accessories, before you visit the showroom.

It is best to go to local, well-established, reputable dealers. If you buy a car outside your community, the problem of getting good quick service is almost sure to develop. If you buy from a local dealer, inquire about the service others have had. Maybe you can save a few dollars buying a car out of town, but the available service closer to home is worth paying a little more for.

Shop around the different dealers and compare prices. Don't hesitate to offer less than the dealer asks. He is going to make all the profit he can and rightly so, but don't let him make it all on you. Don't let a salesman talk you into buying a car that costs more than you can afford. You have already established a ceiling – don't go over it.

After you have decided which car and which dealer you want, a written agreement must be made. Be sure everything you want is down on paper. When the bill of sale is written up, be sure that the make, model, year, equipment, and all accessories are noted. If you are not taking the car right away, make sure that the delivery date is written in. If you are trading a used car, its value should be deducted from the price of the new car on the bill of sale. If sales tax applies in your province, it will be charged on the difference you must pay between your trade-in and your new car. Before you sign the order form or bill of sale, be sure you read it very carefully. Ask your parents for advice if any details confuse you.

Some dealers include the licence for the car in the price, but if not, you will have to pay the cost yourself. Try to persuade the dealer to throw this item in before you close the deal.

If the dealer asks for an advance payment, be sure to get a receipt for it, with the remaining balance noted. The receipt should be signed by him or by his authorized representative. Remember that the dealer does not have to refund your advance payment if you decide not to buy the car.

When the car is ready, check it over thoroughly before you take delivery, to be sure that you have everything you ordered. If not, do not accept the car until the situation is corrected.

Before you leave the dealership, have the service policy of the car explained thoroughly by the service manager, so you will know your responsibility for servicing the car to protect it, you, and your warranty.

Read the owner's manual and the warranty policy. If you have any questions, be sure to find the answers. Be sure to obtain the registration of the vehicle, your insurance policy, and your insurance liability certificate. The first and last of these items must be with you whenever you drive.

If you drive properly, and service your car regularly, it will give you years of good service.

BUYING A USED CAR

If you cannot afford a new car, the alternative is to buy a used one. Used cars can be very good, or very bad, or somewhere in between. Prices range from $100.00 to $6,000.00 or even higher. Again, however, you must not exceed the maximum financial load you can safely or economically afford.

When buying a used car, take it through a diagnostic lane before purchase.
The minimal charge can save a costly error

Where To Buy

Used cars can be purchased from a dealer, from used-car lots, or through private deals.

Usually a well-established dealer is the best choice. Many used-car lots are very reputable, however, as long as they are well-established in the community and have acquired a good reputation for fair prices, a good warranty, good service, and good quality cars. Private deals may save you some money, but usually no warranty is given, which means that you are definitely taking a chance. A private deal between two citizens may also encounter such difficulties as financial liens, stolen cars, and mechanical problems. Any one of these circumstances could cause undue worry and expense.

What To Look For

When buying a used car, it is a great asset to have a good knowledge of automotive mechanics. Even if you do not, however, there are certain pointers which are always helpful to keep in mind.

First of all, don't put too much faith in the indicated number of miles that the car has travelled. Sometimes an adjustment of the odometer reading is made by the vendor, to indicate fewer miles than the car has actually been driven. A car two or three years old may have seventy or eighty thousand miles on it, yet only indicate twenty or thirty thousand.

Do not be misled by a sharp-looking car. It may be worn out mechanically. It is nice to have a car that looks good, but don't let that be the sole deciding factor.

When you have shopped around and found a car that is the proper size, is properly equipped, and looks dependable, ask the salesman for the name of the person who owned the car previously. Contact that person if possible, and get the history of the car. Is the mileage on the odometer correct? Has it been in a collision, and if so, how badly was it damaged? What trouble has he or she had with it? Why did he sell it? Most people will be honest with you.

If you cannot find the previous owner, then you must use other means of deciding whether or not to buy the car. If you are not familiar with automobiles, it is a good idea to have the car checked by a competent certified mechanic, or else take it through a diagnostic lane for an inspection. This service may cost about $10.00

or so, but it may save you hundreds of dollars in repairs already needed or developing.

By all means road test the car before you purchase it, and look at some of the tell-tale facts about the car. Is the body in good repair, with no dents, rust, or body parts loose or falling off? Are there any recently-painted panels or indications of collision damage? The front seat should not be worn or sagged, or the pedals severely worn — these signs are indicators of a lot of use. Has there been a taxi-radio antenna on the roof? How does the car steer in the city or on the highway? Do the brakes operate evenly and stop efficiently? Are the body and chassis tight, or do they rattle? Look at the instrument gauges for indications of malfunctioning. How does the engine operate? Is it smooth and quiet, or does it make noises or run unevenly at different speeds and under different load-conditions? Does it start quickly? Is the exhaust system quiet and are there any odours of oil, gas, or exhaust fumes when it is cold or hot? Look at the chassis and the underneath parts of the car. Observe oil leaks at the engine, transmission, and differential. Check the exhaust visually for leaks or signs of weakness. Check the springs and shocks for breakage or looseness, and the suspension parts for wear or damage. Look at the tires for good tread and even wear, and don't forget the spare and the jack. Uneven tire-wear indicates suspension and steering conditions which are expensive to repair.

Check the safety items such as the inside and outside mirrors. Make sure there is no broken or cracked glass. Check the seat belts and seat belt anchor-bolts in the floor — the latter may be rusted out of the floor pan. Check the seat adjuster, the door locks, and the hinges.

Car dealers spend four or five hours cleaning a car to make it look good, and to cover up any obvious signs that it was poorly cared for. If the engine looks clean on top, look at the bottom — they do not wash the bottom of the motor.

After you have had the car inspected, if you think the price is fair, ask the dealer to make any repairs that you feel are needed as a condition for your purchase. If he refuses to make the repairs — he can't afford to and so neither can you. If this happens, look somewhere else for another car.

Some provinces require a "Mechanical Fitness Certificate" which must be completed before the car can be sold. Whether you are

DATE OF INSPECTION

CERTIFICATE OF MECHANICAL FITNESS
Issued pursuant to Section 49 of The Highway Traffic Act

PARTICULARS OF USED MOTOR VEHICLE

MAKE .... YEAR .... TYPE ....

REGISTRATION PLATE NO. .... YEAR .... SERIAL NUMBER ....

I HEREBY CERTIFY that the above described motor vehicle has been examined in accordance with the provisions of Section 49 of The Highway Traffic Act and Regulation 354/68 and that the items inspected met the prescribed requirements and performance standards on the date of inspection.

*Signature of Selling Dealer .... Address ....

Licence Number of Dealer ....

**Signature of Motor Mechanic .... Address ....
holding a subsisting certificate of qualification as a motor mechanic under the Apprenticeship and Tradesmen's Qualification Act, 1964.

Number of Certificate ....
*may be signed by a dealer in respect of a used motor vehicle being sold by him.
**in all other cases the Certificate of Mechanical Fitness must be signed by a motor mechanic holding a subsisting certificate of qualification as a motor mechanic under the Apprenticeship and Tradesmen's Qualification Act, 1964.
Every person who makes a false statement in a Certificate of Mechanical Fitness is guilty of an offence and on summary conviction is liable to a fine of not more than $300.
VALID FOR 30 DAYS AFTER DATE OF INSPECTION

FORWARD THIS COPY TO DEPARTMENT OF
TRANSPORTATION AND COMMUNICATIONS ONTARIO

LIST OF INSPECTIONS

Passenger Cars and Dual Purpose Vehicles,

Commercial Vehicles

1. Bodywork, Lamps and Reflectors
2. Engine Compartment
3. Mirrors and Seating
4. Glazing Materials
5. Windshield Wiper and Defroster
6. Lighting Equipment Operation
7. Steering Column and Horn
8. Steering Wheel Play and Jamming
9. Service Brake Operation

10. Parking Brake Operation
11. Front Suspension Misalignment and Wear
12. Steering Linkage
13. Tires
14. Wheels and Hubs
15. Brakes—Drums and Discs
16. Brakes—Friction Materials
17. Brakes—Hydraulic and Mechanical Components
18. Chassis Frame and Underbody Components
19. Exhaust Muffler and Underbody Components
20. Fuel System, Drive Shaft and U-Joints
21. Headlamp Aim
22. Service Brake Performance Test

Commercial Vehicles (trucks, truck tractors, trailers)

Complete inspections 1 through 22 as for passenger car, plus the following:

23C. Couplings and Connectors
24C. Air System Components
25C. Vacuum Components
26C. Electric Brake System Components
27C. Trailer Emergency Brakes

Motorcycles

28M. Headlamp and Tail Lamp
29M. Tires
30M. Steering
31M. Brakes
32M. Exhaust System
33M. Bodywork

selling or buying a car, this certificate stating the car is safe for the roads must be submitted before the registration can be transferred from one owner to the other.

Before you purchase the car, discuss the warranty the dealer will honour. No matter what the warranty, be sure you get it in writing. Warranties range from none (be careful of this situation; if the car isn't warrantable, it probably isn't worth buying) to 100 per cent for a stipulated time or mileage, whichever occurs first. For example, 100 per cent of the cost of any repairs is payable by the dealer for 90 days or 4,000 miles; or 30 days or 1,000 miles; or whatever the specified period may be. An alternative arrangement is the "50-50" warranty, whereby you pay half the cost of repairs and the dealer pays the other half during the period the warranty is in force.

As a final word on the subject of used cars — if you can't afford a good used car, then you definitely can't afford to buy a bad one. A worn-out car means endless expense and trouble, and will cost you far more in the long run.

FINANCING A CAR PURCHASE

Credit financing is common today. By paying cash for a new or used car, however, you will probably save money on the initial deal, and of course, save the interest on the loan. Pay cash if you can.

Do not exceed your budget limits because a high pressure salesman argues that the difference would only add a few more dollars a month to the cost. If you are unable to meet the payments, your car may be re-possessed — which means that you lose your car and all the money you have paid on it. And don't forget that when you buy the car you need not only the initial investment, but also enough money for insurance and operating costs. The initial price of the vehicle is only the start of the cost of owning a car.

Most dealers and used-car lots have "on-the-spot" financing for convenience. The dealer often gets a rebate for selling a financial contract for a loan company, so he may try to persuade you to finance through him. You may be able to get a better loan from another source, however. When you purchase a car, you shop around; when you need money, shop around also — the rates are different. Loans are available from banks, loan companies, car dealers, credit unions, and private individuals. Legislation states that all loans must state the interest rate and the total cost on the contract. Loans may cost up to 24 per cent depending on the company and the security you can furnish. Therefore, be sure you investigate loan costs from several sources and get the most inexpensive one.

A minor cannot sign a contract for financial aid without a co-signer or parental approval. Any failure on your behalf to meet the payments will then automatically become the responsibility of your parents or the co-signer. Always re-pay loans on time; by doing so you will establish a good credit rating, which means that any future loans can be obtained at a lower rate of interest.

20

maintaining your car

Any appreciable investment is worth protecting. A car is a major entry in anyone's budget, and to protect it against unsafe mechanical conditions, premature wear, and poor economy, the owner should establish an efficient maintenance program. Fleet owners, for instance, invariably have a regular service program for all their vehicles, whether cars or trucks. They know from experience that regular inspections save time and money, and reduce accidents due to mechanical failures. It is also an obligation and moral responsibility to operate a safe car on public roads.

The best guide for the care and preventive maintenance of a car is to follow the recommendations prescribed by the manufacturer as outlined in the owner's manual. If the car is purchased used, a replacement manual can probably be obtained from the dealer or from the manufacturer. In any case, the information in the following pages of this chapter will give you a good idea of the requirements for properly maintaining your car.

Service requirements can be divided into two groups: regular inspections and periodic inspections and adjustments. Each of these will be considered separately below.

REGULAR INSPECTIONS

Each time the car is refuelled at a service station, several checks should be made, Always ask for these checks to be done — not every service station will perform all the required inspections because it is time consuming. These are the checks that should be performed:

1. Regular service begins with filling the tank with gas. Do not buy a premium fuel if it is not needed for your engine. No advantage will be gained in economy or performance if your car has a low-compression engine. On the other hand, if you have a high-compression engine, using a regular-grade fuel will cause a "carbon build-up," loss of power, and other related malfunctions. Try to keep the gas tank above the one-quarter level to prevent water from condensing in the gasoline.

2. Have the engine oil-level checked; add oil when — and only when — the dipstick under the hood indicates the need. Let the engine stand (not running) for two or three minutes before checking. This allows the oil to drip into the oil pan. If oil is needed, add the same type as is already in the engine.

3. Check the condition of the fan, generator or alternator, and power-steering belts. If the belts are worn, frayed, or cracked, they should be replaced; this only takes a few minutes. The fan belt is very important because it operates the cooling-system fan and the water pump, and also drives the generator or alternator to charge the battery and operate the electrical equipment. The power-steering belt drives the hydraulic pump to operate the power steering. If the belt or belts are loose, have them adjusted so they will drive the units at the proper speed without slipping.

4. Check the battery water-level. If the water level should go too low, serious damage and early failure of the battery will result. If the battery uses excessive amounts of water, have it checked for leaks, and also check that the charging rate of the generator is not too high.

5. Check the water or anti-freeze level. If the radiator is low, have the cooling system checked for leaks. Be sure to add anti-freeze instead of water during the winter months — a frozen cooling system will virtually ruin an engine.

6. Fill the windshield reservoir with water, or with anti-freeze solution during cold weather.

7. Check the tire pressure. Don't forget to check the spare. The front tires usually need higher pressure than the rear, because they must support the weight of the engine. The spare should have the same pressure as the front tires, so that it can be used on either the front or the rear. Adjust the tire pressure according to manufacturer's specifications. Normal tire pressure allows the total tread-area to contact the road, thus giving good traction and the best tire wear. Under-inflation causes the tire to recede in the centre, so that wear increases on the outer edges, thereby reducing tire life and traction. Over-inflation causes the tire to contact the road in the centre of the tread due to a bulge in the tire. This also causes rapid tire-wear and less traction. Tire pressure should not be adjusted when the tires are hot. Heat increases the pressure in the tire, and therefore distorts the reading taken with the pressure gauge. Check the tire-wear patterns and tread depth. If tread is less than one-sixteenth of an inch deep, have the tires replaced. If the tires on the front are

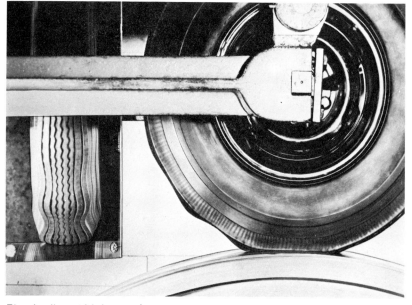

Tire rippling at high speed

Tires should be replaced when tread is less than 1/16 of an inch deep

wearing on the edges of the tread, this indicates either excessive under-inflation, or that the front wheels need to be aligned.

8. Check the brake master-cylinder fluid level. If the level is down, have the system checked for leaks and repaired immediately.
9. Clean the windshield, rear window, and outside rear view mirror for best vision.
10. Check all the lights for operation, including the headlights, both upper and lower beam; parking lights; side lights; tail and licence-plate lights; stop lights; signal lights; hazard-flashing lights; and interior lights. Failure to see, to be seen, and to communicate with other drivers and pedestrians, is a dangerous condition. Light bulbs can burn out anytime; check them regularly.

It is best to deal with one service station which has competent, honest employees and management. They will get to know you and your car, and will generally take an interest in both.

Care of the car body is also important to reduce rust, corrosion, and paint discolouring, and to improve general appearance. The car should be washed every week and more often during the winter, when salt is used on the roads. Polishing and waxing the car also protects the finish; it is most advantageous to wax a car every six months — in the spring and in the fall.

Special petroleum-base undercoatings can be applied to the underbody to resist rust. Ask your dealer about this treatment — you will probably find it is well worth the money.

A clean car seems to run better — try it!

PERIODIC INSPECTIONS AND ADJUSTMENTS

Once again, the best source of recommendations is the owner's manual. Check it carefully, follow it faithfully, and trouble-free and safe motoring will be yours to enjoy. The information in the following paragraphs will also be helpful to explain the most common procedures and operations, and the time and/or mileage intervals at which they should be done.

Changing The Oil

Changing the engine oil should be done ideally at two thousand miles or every two months, whichever first occurs. Dirt, sludge, water, and fine pieces of metal mix with the oil; unless the oil is changed regularly, these contaminants will eventually cause the formation of gum and varnish, which may plug the oil circuits in the engine. This will prevent the oil from reaching vital moving parts, resulting in wear, noise, and expensive repair bills. The oil filter removes most of the dirt, and must be replaced every six thousand miles or six months. Constant freeway driving is less contaminating for the oil, and oil-change intervals can therefore be extended.

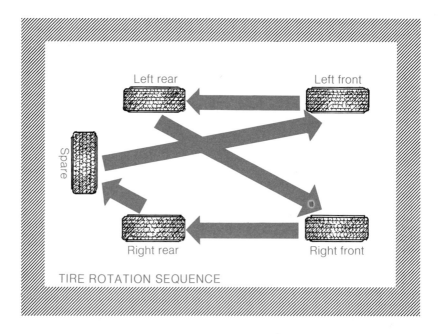

TIRE ROTATION SEQUENCE

Rotating The Tires

Rotating the tires — that is, changing the location of each tire including the spare — gives the best mileage possible from all the tires. This operation should be performed every six thousand miles.

Cleaning The Battery Cables

The most frequent cause of a car's failing to start is corrosion of the battery cables and terminals. These should be removed, cleaned, and tightened every six months or six thousand miles. It's good starting insurance!

Fluid-Levels And Lubrication

Check the fluid-levels in the brake master-cylinder, power-steering pump, transmission (standard or automatic), the differential, and the radiator. Each unit has its own unique type of liquid, grease, or fluid, and occasionally evaporation and leakage makes it necessary to fill them to the proper level. Never over-fill, and always use the proper fluid — substitutes may cause serious damage.

Most modern cars have extended chassis and front-suspension lubrication intervals. However, the lubrication points should be greased at approximately 24,000 miles. Each manufacturer is somewhat different, but failure to lubricate the suspension will result in excessive wear.

Light lubrication of door locks, hinges, hood and trunk locks and hinges, gearshift linkages and parking-brake cables, will reduce rust, prevent seizing, and promote smooth operation.

Tune-Ups

The common operation of "tuning-up an engine" probably has as many definitions as there are drivers and garages. An engine-service operation check every ten to twelve thousand miles is a necessity, and must cover all the engine auxiliary systems to assure continued economical and efficient operation. The ignition must be checked extensively; usually the spark plugs will need replacing at this mileage. The fuel and cooling systems must be thoroughly checked also. Ask your mechanic exactly what he does for a tune-up; if it does not seem sufficiently thorough, take him the chart on page 226 and

Maintenance operations	Mileage and/or months intervals (thousands of miles)						
Note: always check manufacturer's specifications	2	6	12	18	24	30	36
Change engine oil	X						
Change engine oil filter		X	X	X	X	X	X
Rotate tires		X	X	X	X		
Remove and clean battery cable connectors		X	X	X	X	X	X
Check fluid levels: brakes, radiator, transmission, differential, power-steering pump		X	X	X	X	X	X
Lubricate: door locks, hinges, hood and trunk lock and hinges, parking-brake cables, gearshift linkage, bumper jack		X	X	X	X	X	X
Engine tune-up: test compression; replace spark plugs; test spark plug wires; remove, inspect, and lubricate distributor; replace points if necessary; test condenser; set ignition timing; test coil output; test fuel pump pressure and volume; replace fuel filter(s); replace air filter element (paper type); test P.C.V. system and replace valve if necessary; clean crankcase breather; adjust carburetor-speed and mixture; check emission control system; free the heat riser valve pressure; test the cooling system; test battery; check charging-circuit output; blow out dirt from radiator core; test starter current draw; adjust automatic trans. linkage; wash engine; inspect for oil leaks; road test for proper operation under all conditions [1]			X		X		X
Check front end alignment, wheel balance, steering, shocks		X	X	X	X	X	X
Aim headlights			X		X		X
Check brake lines and linings			X	X			X
Remove, clean, inspect, lubricate and adjust front wheel bearings					X		
Lubricate universal joints						X	
Change automatic transmission fluid and clean filter					X		
Replace radiator coolant and anti-freeze					X		
Lubricate and check front suspension ball joints					X		
Report any abnormal condition and have it checked immediately	ANYTIME						

[1] Not necessarily in the proper sequence

ask him to perform all these operations and report his findings. If he doesn't do so, take the car where they will. This must be done for your protection.

Alignment And Balancing

The front-wheel alignment must be watched very carefully. A front wheel out of alignment can wear a tire smooth in 5,000 miles or even less. If a tire shows wear on one side of the tread, have the front wheels aligned. The front suspension can be put out of alignment by hitting curbs, going too fast over holes in the road, or through collision. Driving slowly over severe bumps or holes will reduce alignment problems, and of course, keeping the wheels off the side of a curb will also help.

Wheel imbalance is a condition which causes the car to shake or vibrate at highway speeds. A tire out of balance wears unevenly if it is left unbalanced for any length of time. Imbalance is also detrimental to the suspension parts, especially the springs and shocks. Have the balance checked whenever the tires are rotated, or when the front-wheel alignment is checked.

Wheel alignment

Wheel balancing

Headlights

The headlights are mounted on springs to reduce breakage and to provide a means of adjustment. A special machine is required to adjust the headlights so that they aim correctly. Too high a light will blind oncoming drivers, and does not show the road surface. A light that is too low does not illuminate your "danger zone" at highway speeds.

Brakes And Wheel Bearings

Due to friction, heat, and wear, the brake linings on all the wheels will eventually wear thin. Careful inspection of both front and rear brake linings, brake lines, and hydraulic cylinders is suggested at 12,000 miles and each 6,000 miles thereafter. Usually a brake-overhaul is not needed until about 20,000 miles or so, but an extended amount of city driving increases the wear rate of the brakes. Never take a chance on brakes. Always use good quality parts and a competent repairman for this operation.

The front wheel-bearings need inspection, lubrication, and adjustment to provide adequate protection against wheel seizure or loose front wheels. Have them inspected at least every 24,000 miles.

The Transmission

The automatic transmission should have its fluid changed, the sump pan cleaned, and the filter cleaned to insure proper lubrication and operation, and to prevent tiny metal particles from affecting the intricate valves. Some automatics need the bands adjusted at this time — check your manual or dealer.

The Radiator

The coolant, usually anti-freeze solution in the radiator, will protect the system against rust and corrosion for about two years. After this period, it must be changed. And to emphasize once again — never begin a winter without testing the anti-freeze.

If any abnormal condition exists in the vehicle at any time, such as a noise, vibration, control-difficulty, or failure of any unit to function, have it checked by an expert. It's usually less expensive to fix it now than later. A well-cared-for car is a safe car; a safe car is a good car.

SEASONAL REQUIREMENTS

In the fall, several safety items should be acquired or checked.

Put snow tires on the drive wheels. Check provincial legislation regarding the use of studs in tires. Steel or tungsten-studded tires give added traction on ice under certain conditions. They are hard on the road surfaces, however, and some provinces restrict their use to certain winter months. Other provinces do not allow them at all.

A shovel, a little box of sand, chains, and traction pads are handy items to have in the trunk for emergency use if you get stuck.

In the fall, don't forget to check the exhaust system for leaks, and check the anti-freeze in the radiator and windshield washer.

Have an ice scraper handy, and clean *all* the windows of snow and ice so that you can see all around your car.

EMERGENCY EQUIPMENT

A conscientious, safe, defensive driver always expects the unexpected. Sometimes emergencies occur and you are happy to have the necessary equipment readily available. If you do not, you usually wish you had.

Every car should have a traveller's first-aid kit, which can be purchased in drug stores or department stores very reasonably. A dry-chemical fire extinguisher is desirable for gasoline and electrical fires which occasionally happen. An extra fan belt and a small tool-kit will help if you are on a freeway and the belt breaks. A fan belt is easy to replace, inexpensive, and vital.

A flashlight is handy for many purposes, routine as well as emergency. Keep it in the glove compartment – and always have good batteries in it!

Keep some spare fuses for the electrical circuits and ask your mechanic to show you their location. If the tail lights, heater, or instruments fail due to a fuse failure, it is best to be prepared.

A white cloth should be kept in the car for attaching to the radio antenna or door handle as an emergency signal. It is also useful for cleaning your hands, windshield, or anything else when required.

Be sure you know where the car jack is located, how it works, and the correct procedure for jacking your car. Check the owner's manual for your car and adhere to all the safety precautions.

21

the manual-shift transmission

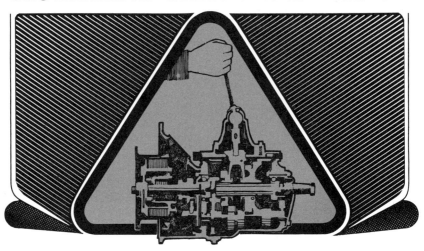

In Chapter 18, the operation of the automatic transmission was discussed. In this chapter, we shall deal with the *manual-shift* transmission, which is found in most trucks, in many imported cars, and in some North American cars as well.

The manual transmission provides a positive mechanical connection between the engine and drive wheels with no slippage. Because there is no slippage — as would be provided by the fluid coupling in an automatic transmission — a special device must be available to interrupt the power flow to provide a momentary neutral and to allow for the changing of gears. This device is called the clutch. The operation of the clutch will be explained in the next section.

THE CLUTCH ASSEMBLY

The clutch assembly is attached to the flywheel, which is the power-output point of the engine. The flywheel has a smooth surface on the backward-facing side so that the clutch plate can engage with it. The clutch disc is attached to the transmission "input" shaft. Whenever the disc is held tightly to the rotating flywheel it is forced to rotate also and it must then turn the transmission shaft and gears.

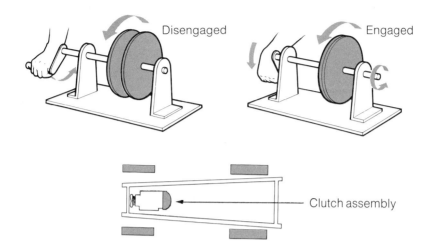

Disengaged

Engaged

Clutch assembly

To hold the clutch disc tightly against the flywheel, a third member is needed, called a pressure plate. The pressure plate is also bolted to the flywheel and turns with it whenever the engine and flywheel are running. The pressure plate has a series of very strong springs which, when released, exert a great pressure on the clutch plate to force it tightly against the rotating flywheel so that it will drive the transmission gears. The driver can disengage the clutch and interrupt the power flow by pushing on the clutch pedal. This action uses leverage to compress the springs in the pressure plate, so that the clutch plate no longer presses against the flywheel, and thus no power is delivered to the transmission.

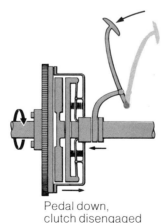

Pedal down,
clutch disengaged

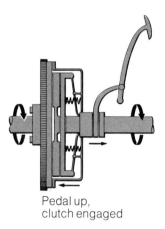

Pedal up,
clutch engaged

When the clutch pedal is "out" or "engaged," there should be about one inch of free pedal-play to take up any slack in the linkage; this must be present to insure positive engagement of the clutch. "Riding the clutch" — that is, keeping the left foot on the clutch pedal unnecessarily after the car is in motion — defeats the purpose of the free-play adjustment, and causes premature failure of the clutch assembly. Never ride the clutch — keep your foot off it when you are not using it.

When a driver is learning to operate a manual-shift transmission, reference is usually made to the "friction point" of the clutch. When the clutch pedal is depressed and the transmission is in gear, let the clutch out *slowly*; about one-third of the way out, the engine speed will decrease, and the car may start to edge slowly forward. It is at this point that the clutch plate contacts the flywheel to transmit engine power; this is the "point of contact" or the "friction point." Further engagement of the clutch must be accompanied by gentle pressure on the accelerator, so that the engine will have sufficient power to start moving the vehicle. Otherwise, the engine will stall.

Properly treated, the clutch will require very little service. The free-play adjustment should be checked and adjusted about every 5,000 miles, or whenever the free-play diminishes.

THE GEAR TRAIN

The manual transmission provides a reverse gear for backing the vehicle, a neutral gear so the engine can run with the clutch engaged without power being transmitted to the rear wheels, and three or four gears, depending on the type of car, for driving forward.

The question arises — why do we need three or four forward gears? The answer is that the different gears provide a mechanical advantage for the engine to the rear wheels. The engine has very little power at slow speeds, and since the car can weigh as much as two tons, to start it moving may be too great a task for the engine. By the use of the lower gears, however, the engine's power can be augmented several times, thereby enabling the car to pull away. Once the car is moving, its momentum aids the engine, and thus the engine speed can be reduced to the same speed as the differential drive-gear, as is the case in high gear.

The transmission consists of a cast iron or aluminum case which houses all the gears and shafts. It is filled with grease or oil to lubricate the moving parts. It is bolted to the rear of the engine behind the clutch assembly. A linkage connects the gearshift lever to the transmission.

Gears of different diameters, when meshed together, are used to increase or decrease rotating speeds. For example, in the above illustration a small gear with 12 teeth is driving a larger gear with 24 teeth. When the small gear turns a distance of 12 teeth, the large gear must turn a distance of 12 teeth also — but this means that while

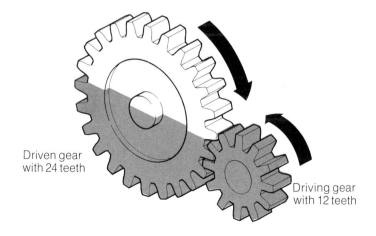

Driven gear
with 24 teeth

Driving gear
with 12 teeth

the small gear has completed one turn, the large gear has completed only one-half a turn. If the gears were each fastened to a separate shaft, the second or larger gear and its shaft would always travel at one-half the speed of the small gear. A decrease of half the speed for the larger gear gives it twice the power or "torque" or twisting ability. If the small gear were connected to the engine, and the larger gear connected to the rear wheels, it would allow the engine to go faster, and so have more power (since it would be operating in a more efficient speed-range); the rear wheels would turn more slowly, but would have a greater torque or turning force to get the car moving.

On the other hand, if a large gear turns a small gear, the small gear will turn more quickly but will have correspondingly weaker torque.

In the automobile transmission, several combinations of gears are used to meet varying load and speed conditions.

For low or first gear, a small gear driven by the engine and clutch drives a large gear on another shaft. This reduces the speed and increases the twisting or turning force. Then a small gear on the second shaft drives a large gear on the drive shaft which goes to the rear axle. This reduces the speed and increases the torque still more, giving a gear ratio of about three-to-one for starting to move the car or for heavy pulling.

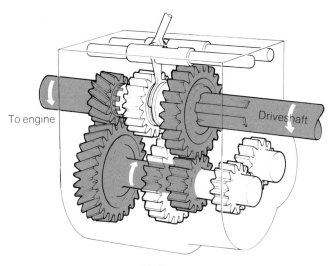

To engine

Driveshaft

First gear

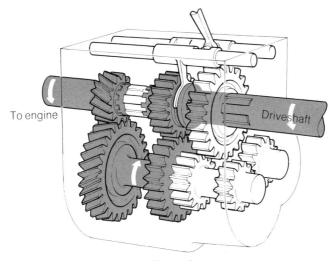

Second gear

When the car has started to move, we need less twisting force to turn the rear wheels, and would like more speed. For second gear, we use the same first pair of gears as in low. We disconnect the second pair and use two other gears. These are arranged with the larger one driving the smaller, so there is less overall speed-reduction than in low gear. The gear train now has an overall gear ratio of about two-to-one.

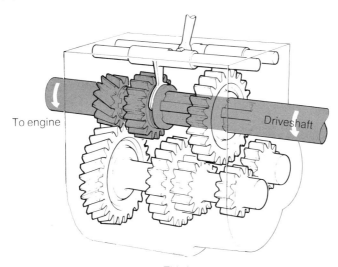

Third gear

Once a car speed of about 25 miles per hour or so is reached, no reduction in the transmission is necessary because engine speed and vehicle momentum are great enough to keep the car moving. A shift to third or high gear connects the engine directly to the propeller shaft and rear axle. They both revolve at the same speed, at a ratio of one-to-one.

For cars with four-speed or even five-speed transmissions, the principle is exactly the same — there are simply more intermediate gears to be shifted. The additional gears enable the car to accelerate somewhat more rapidly; these transmissions are usually found on sports cars.

Reverse gear is very much like low gear, with about the same gear ratio (three-to-one), using the same four gears. Reverse uses a fifth gear which causes the drive shaft to turn in the opposite direction to the engine.

Neutral disengages all gears except the first pair; therefore, no power is transferred to the rear axle.

Three-speed gearshift positions are usually of the "H" design. The most common location of the three-speed gearshift lever is under the steering column. Viewed from the passenger's seat, the pattern would look like an "H" on its side (see diagram).

Four-speed gearshifts have an "H" pattern also, except that the four corners of the "H" represent the four forward speeds. The

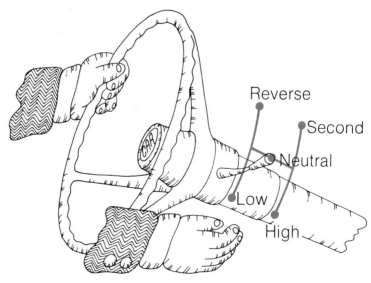

reverse position varies from car to car, but there is usually a diagram on the gearshift knob indicating its location. The gearshift lever for four-speed transmission is usually located on the console to the right of the driver's seat; in some cars, however, it is found under the steering column just like a three-speed shift.

To change from any one gear to another, remove your foot from the accelerator, depress the clutch pedal with the left foot, move the gearshift lever to neutral and then to the desired gear, gently release the clutch, and return your right foot to the accelerator pedal.

Before you attempt to drive a standard transmission car, be sure you read the following section on "Driving the Stick Shift."

DRIVING THE STICK SHIFT

Driving with a manual-shift transmission is somewhat different than with an automatic. There are skills which must be correctly developed to move the car smoothly through the gear ratios for varying load and power conditions, without stalling the engine, jerking the car, or causing undue wear. Three factors must be considered almost simultaneously when using a gearshift: gearshift selection and movement; clutch skill; and accelerator application. These three operations must be performed without the necessity of looking at what you are doing, because you must steer the car and always be watching the road and traffic conditions.

Gearshift Selection

First let us look at the gearshift. To simplify the explanation, in this section we shall discuss only the three-speed shift; the basic operation of the four-speed is very much the same, however.

Before driving the car, practise moving the gearshift through the various positions in its pattern, with the engine off. To begin, before shifting any gear you must always depress the clutch pedal. Turn the palm of your right hand up towards the steering wheel when shifting into low or reverse gears, and the palm of your right hand down when shifting to second or high. This will tend automatically to cause you to lift the gearshift for low and reverse through neutral, and to push the lever down slightly for second and high.

Once you have the feel of the gearshift pattern, try the procedures in the following exercises. Be sure to have a qualified instructor who can help.

STARTING THE ENGINE

1. Put the parking brake on.
2. Depress the clutch pedal to the floor with your left foot.
3. Move the gearshift lever to the neutral position.
4. Set the automatic choke by quickly depressing the accelerator and then releasing it with the right foot.
5. Start the engine.
6. The clutch can be *slowly* released, and the car should not move. If it tries to move, the gearshift is not in neutral. Shut the engine off and try again.

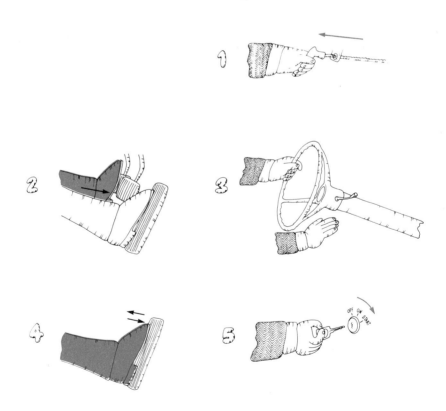

MOVING THE CAR

Before you move the car, know how to stop it! Find the brake and test it with your right foot. Start the engine, and then begin the exercise.

1. Depress the clutch with your left foot.
2. Shift to low gear, keeping the palm of your right hand up.
3. Release the parking brake.
4. Check your mirror and your blind spot for traffic.
5. Signal that you are starting up.
6. Press the accelerator to speed up the engine a little, and let the clutch out, *slowly*, until the "point of contact" or "friction point" is felt. The engine may start to slow down at this point.
7. Slowly let the clutch pedal up, and . . .
8. Accelerate lightly at the same time. Keep your eyes up!

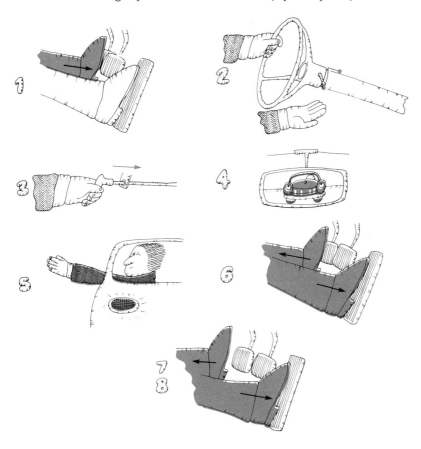

STOPPING THE CAR

1. Check the traffic.
2. Signal a stop.
3. Depress the clutch first (in low gear and reverse only).
4. Release the accelerator immediately after depressing the clutch.
5. Apply the brake with your right foot, bringing the car to a stop.
6. Shift to neutral.
7. Apply the parking brake, and remove your feet from the pedals slowly.
8. Turn off the engine. Leave the gearshift in low or in reverse gear if you leave the car.

SHIFTING FROM LOW TO SECOND

As your speed increases, you must shift from low to second, and then to high gear. Be sure you keep your eyes up, watch the traffic, and be ready for any emergency.

1. When the car has reached about 10 miles per hour, a shift to second is needed.
2. Depress the clutch, and almost at the same time . . .
3. Release the accelerator.
4. With your palm down, push the gearshift lever to neutral and on up to second gear.
5. Release the clutch slowly, especially through the friction point, and at the same time . . .
6. Gently press the accelerator.

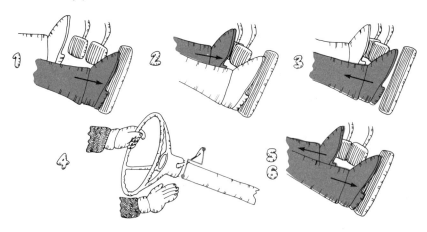

SHIFTING FROM SECOND TO HIGH

1. Accelerate in second to about 20 miles per hour.
2. Keeping your eyes ahead, depress the clutch and release the accelerator.
3. With your palm down, shift to high gear.
4. Let the clutch pedal come up smoothly but quickly, and at the same time, press on the accelerator.
5. Move your left foot off the clutch pedal and place it on the floor.

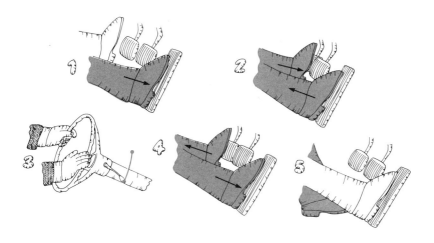

STOPPING IN HIGH GEAR

Stopping in high gear is different from stopping in low — you release the accelerator first, and then disengage the clutch.

1. Check the traffic, using both mirror and shoulder checks.
2. Signal for a stop.
3. Release the accelerator.
4. Apply the brake and slow the car to about 10 miles per hour.
5. Depress the clutch pedal.
6. Continue braking, easing up slightly just before the car comes to a stop.
7. Move the gearshift lever to neutral.
8. If stopping to park, apply the parking brake, turn off the engine, put the gearshift in low or reverse, and release the clutch.

SHIFTING FROM HIGH TO SECOND

Occasionally — on hills, slowing down in traffic, or turning corners — it is necessary to downshift from high to second. Do not downshift at a speed that is not normal for the second gear, but reduce the car's speed with the brakes first. Downshifting on ice or snow can be dangerous; let the clutch out very slowly through the friction point.

1. Release the accelerator, and brake if necessary to reduce speed.
2. Depress the clutch pedal.
3. Shift from high to second.
4. Press the accelerator and bring the engine speed up to that of the second-gear range.
5. Release the clutch slowly, and adjust the accelerator according to what you are going to do: if you are driving up a hill, press down on the accelerator; if you are slowing to a stop, release the accelerator.

BACKING UP

1. Depress the clutch.
2. With your palm up, shift to reverse by lifting the lever and moving it away from you.
3. Check traffic.
4. Press on the accelerator slightly, and at the same time . . .
5. Slowly let the clutch out to the "point of contact," and the car will begin to move.

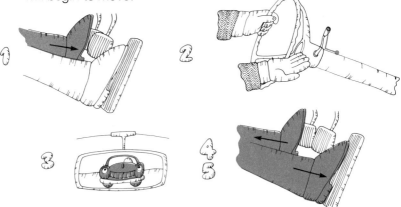

STARTING ON AN UPGRADE

Occasionally you will have to stop part way up a steep hill. Do not allow the car to roll back when you start off again. To avoid this, put the parking brake on, let the clutch pedal out to the friction point and then release the parking brake. Increase pressure on the accelerator to keep the car moving as you fully release the clutch. Be sure you know how to do this operation, but do not attempt it until you have had sufficient experience with a clutch and a standard transmission.

1. Stop the car at the right side of the road after checking the traffic and signalling. Be sure to depress the clutch to prevent stalling.
2. Put the parking brake fully on so it will hold the car. If you need to use your left foot for the brake, shift to neutral first and then apply the brake.
3. Shift to low gear.
4. Keep your right hand on the steering wheel; signal, and check the traffic.

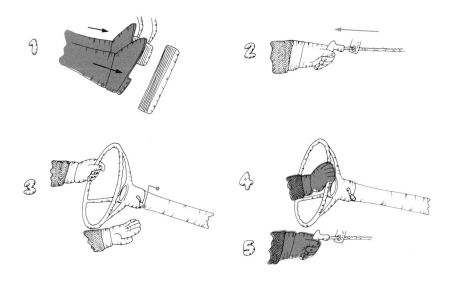

5. Put your left hand on the parking-brake, ready to release it.
6. Press the accelerator sufficiently to start the car on a hill, release the clutch to the friction point, and wait until the car tries to

move. Then release the parking brake and continue to accelerate.

7. Fully release the clutch and brake, and accelerate to a speed which will allow a shift to second gear.

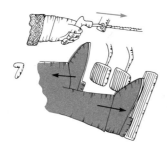
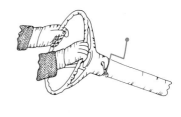

PARKING THE CAR

When leaving a car parked, follow the same procedure as with an automatic, except leave the transmission in low or reverse gear.

1. Apply the parking brake.
2. Depress the clutch, and shift to low or reverse.
3. Turn off the engine.
4. Remove the key.
5. Release the clutch.
6. Check traffic, exit, and lock the doors.

PUSH-STARTING YOUR CAR

Occasionally it is necessary to start a car with a push, due to battery or starter failure. Before you attempt this, be sure the other driver of the pushing car is fully aware of what to do. Be extremely cautious if on ice or slippery pavement. Be sure the bumpers of both cars meet properly to prevent any body damage.

1. Turn the ignition switch to the "on" position.
2. Depress the clutch pedal.
3. Release the parking brake.
4. Shift to second gear.
5. Push to a speed of about 15 miles per hour.
6. Slowly release the clutch; the engine will begin to turn over, and should start almost immediately.
7. When the engine starts, accelerate away from the pushing car. If the car does not start immediately, try it a few more times. If it still fails, call your local mechanic.

STICKSHIFT TIPS

Continued use of a clutch and standard transmission develops a high degree of skill in smooth shifting and efficient driving. You will probably not do it smoothly the first time, but as you practise, you will shift with no grinding of gears and without conscious effort. Particularly, keep the following points in mind:

1. Never slip the clutch to hold a car from rolling backwards on a hill. Always use the brakes to hold the car.
2. When the car is idling at an intersection, always shift to neutral and release the clutch; otherwise, your foot may slip off the clutch pedal, allowing the car to lurch forward and perhaps run over someone. This can easily happen when drivers have snow or mud on their left foot.
3. Do not "ride" a clutch. When the clutch is fully engaged and the car is moving along, take your foot off the pedal completely, and place it on the floor. If you leave your foot even resting on the pedal, it will cause wear to the clutch assembly.
4. Have the clutch free-play adjustment checked about every 5,000 miles of driving.
5. If a car is stuck in mud or snow, "rocking" the car by shifting from low to reverse using the clutch and accelerator will be very effective in getting out.
6. When stopping in high gear or second gear, always leave the clutch engaged until the car slows to about 10 miles per hour. This uses the engine as a brake and saves the foot brakes, and also provides smoother deceleration.
7. When driving slowly in mud and snow or on ice, second gear is usually best if you apply the accelerator gently and easily.

index

Note: page numbers in italic refer to illustrations

in mountains, 112
poor visibility, 140-141
preparing for, 120
push start on ice, 244
rocking the car, 245
slowing down, 66

snow tires, 120, 123, 229
stopping, 89
clearing windshields, 26-27, 115
120, 221
(*see also* anti-freeze)

acknowledgements

The following have contributed to the photographic portion of the text:

American Motors Corp., p. 26
Bill Brooks Photography, pp. 23, 25, 26, 28, 29, 30, 33, 37, 48, 66, 67,
81, 87, 94, 105, 108, 117, 121, 137, 140, 214, 217, 227
Chrysler Corp., pp. 22, 23
Jeep Corp., pp. 24, 30
Miller Services, Richard Harrington photo, p. 218
Ontario Provincial Police, pp. 158, 171
R. C. M. P., p. 169
Rubber Assoc. of Canada, p. 222
Volvo Corp., p. 22